PLURAL POLICING
Theory and practice

Colin Rogers

P

First published in Great Britain in 2017 by

Policy Press
University of Bristol
1-9 Old Park Hill
Bristol
BS2 8BB
UK
t: +44 (0)117 954 5940
pp-info@bristol.ac.uk
www.policypress.co.uk

North America office:
Policy Press
c/o The University of Chicago Press
1427 East 60th Street
Chicago, IL 60637, USA
t: +1 773 702 7700
f: +1 773-702-9756
sales@press.uchicago.edu
www.press.uchicago.edu

© Policy Press 2017

British Library Cataloguing in Publication Data
A catalogue record for this book is available from the British Library

Library of Congress Cataloging-in-Publication Data
A catalog record for this book has been requested

ISBN 978-1-4473-2541-3 paperback
ISBN 978-1-4473-2540-6 hardcover
ISBN 978-1-4473-2542-0 ePub
ISBN 978-1-4473-2543-7 Mobi
ISBN 978-1-4473-2639-7 ePdf

Cover design by Policy Press
Front cover image: www.alamy.com
Printed and bound in Great Britain by CPI Group (UK) Ltd, Croydon, CR0 4YY
Policy Press uses environmentally responsible print partners

KEY THEMES IN POLICING

Series summary: This textbook series is designed to fill a growing need for titles which reflect the importance of incorporating 'evidence based policing' within Higher Education curriculums. It will reflect upon the changing landscape of contemporary policing as it becomes more politicised, professionalised and scrutinised, and draw out both change and continuities in its themes.

Series Editors: Dr Megan O'Neill, University of Dundee, Dr Marisa Silvestri, Kingston University and Dr Stephen Tong, Canterbury Christ Church University.

Published
Understanding police intelligence work – Adrian James

Forthcoming
Practical Psychology for Policing – Dr Jason Roach

Key Challenges in Criminal Investigation – Dr Martin O'Neill

Miscarriages of Justice: Causes, consequences and remedies – Dr Sam Poyser, Dr Angus Nurse and Dr Becky Milne

Editorial advisory board
- Paul Quinton (College of Policing)
- Professor Nick Fyfe (University of Dundee)
- Professor Jennifer Brown (LSE)
- Charlotte E. Gill (George Mason University)

Contents

List of tables, figures and boxes

Tables

Figures

Boxes

Series preface

The Key Themes in Policing series aims to support the growing number of policing modules on both undergraduate and postgraduate courses, as well as contribute to the development of policing professionals, both those new in service and existing practitioners. It also seeks to respond to the call for evidence-based policing led by organisations such as the College of Policing in England. By producing a range of high-quality, research-informed texts on important areas of policing, contributions to the series support and inform both professional and academic policing curriculums.

Representing the second text in the series, Colin Rogers' *Plural Policing* addresses an important topic within contemporary policing research and practice. Considering both the broader historical context as well as contemporary challenges, Colin Rogers charts the development and configuration of pluralised policing. While the police have never been entirely alone in their task of ensuring safety, security and the rule of law, the degree and nature of the policing 'others' has shifted dramatically over time. The publication of this book comes at a time when many are questioning the purpose of policing in light of reduced resources across the public sector.

Colin Rogers is a former police inspector with 30 years' service at South Wales Police and is now a Professor of Police Sciences at the University of South Wales in the Faculty of Life Sciences and Education. He has taught and published extensively on policing and police science, and his work has taken him across the globe to advise several governments and police educational institutions nationally and internationally. In this text, Colin Rogers provides a timely and in-depth analysis of the nature of policing in contemporary society, who performs it and what the future might hold for policing beyond current configurations. Given the ongoing demands of securing 'good' policing against a backdrop of austerity, these are important questions to consider, for both students and practitioners in policing.

Preface

Police organisations across the world are undergoing changes, the details of which, had they discussed less than 10 years ago, would not have been believed. The reduction in the number of official 'sworn' officers, particularly in England and Wales, has produced a debate concerning the role and effectiveness of the police organisation. Societies are now forced to question the value of the traditional public police provision to effectively deal with crime and disorder, in the wake of governments' decisions to reduce budgets, change structures and open up policing to economic market forces.

Not that the use of alternative policing agencies and other 'actors', notably the community themselves, is new. The history of policing illustrates the use of security agencies throughout various time periods, as well as the role of volunteers from within communities. However, in the past these have been used to complement and support the public police in their duties. Today, what we may be witnessing is a change in the role of these other forms of policing. These diverse activities appear to be growing and in some instances replacing the activities formerly undertaken by the public police.

In addition, the political philosophy of 'neoliberalism', within the framework of austerity measures, has provided the opportunity for dramatic change in the way police and policing is considered, especially in England and Wales. In truth, there has been a form of pluralised policing for some years in the shape of neighbourhood policing teams, which draw on a number of different public sector actors and roles to ensure a problem-oriented policing approach takes place. With the dramatic reduction in the number of public police in England and Wales, the structure, form and delivery of neighbourhood policing must surely alter to reflect these changes. Simultaneously, the public police must attempt to deal with more complex national and international demands such as terrorism, internet crime and other global issues that affect national infrastructures.

This book therefore considers the current and future state of the police and policing in England and Wales as it moves towards a more pluralised policing framework. This book is divided into three main sections. The first discusses the complex nature of defining 'the police' and 'policing'. These are two separate concepts, and the distinctions between them need to be fully appreciated before moving on to any consideration of future changes. This section also includes a discussion surrounding the nature of pluralised policing, including a critical discussion surrounding the idea of private policing.

The second section considers the current structures of policing in England and Wales, in particular the neighbourhood policing team approach which includes police community support officers, volunteers and of course the idea of partnership working as a form of pluralised policing.

The final section considers the development of the public police and pluralised policing arrangements that may be seen in the near future, and in particular discusses such issues as the problem of accountability in the context of these coming changes.

The historian David Lowenthal (2011) famously said: 'The past is a foreign country: they do things differently there.' The future may not be a country that is too distant, but in terms of police and policing arrangements, they will definitely be doing things differently there.

Professor Colin Rogers
22 June 2016

Acknowledgements

There are always people who are the unsung heroes behind any work such as this, so it is only right that those individuals be properly acknowledged.

I would like to thank the staff at Policy Press for support and belief, and also patience in dealing with the fact that this book has travelled with me in its compilation for over a year, being partially written in such places as Australia, Brunei, China and Abu Dhabi as well as many European cities as I continue my academic journey. In particular, my thanks go to Rebecca Tomlinson, who has dealt with my requests in such a polite and professional manner.

I also extend my thanks to my family as usual for all of their support, which has been unwavering over the years. In particular, my thanks go to Alice Rogers, who has proved to be an excellent proof reader and grammatical expert and who worked tirelessly to assist me in completing the manuscript. *Diolch, cariad.*

Finally, my thanks go to the police service that was, which helped to develop me for my future.

Part 1
Theory and principles underpinning plural policing

This section examines the theories and principles that underpin the idea of plural policing. It considers the rise of such an approach, reflecting on the social and political pressures that have seen the introduction and acceptance of different agencies becoming involved in activities hitherto only thought to be carried out by the 'public' police.

An important starting point for this section is to discuss just what we mean when we use the terms 'police' and 'policing', as it is important to separate their definitions and understand how they differ from one another. The section will consider the rise in plural policing, private policing and other forms of quasi-policing activity, not just in England and Wales but also in other European countries.

ONE

Who are the police and what is policing?

Introduction: Taking the police out of policing

As Reiner (2010) points out, the term 'police' is primarily used to denote a body of people patrolling public spaces in blue uniforms, with a broad mandate of crime control, order maintenance and some negotiable social service functions. This appears to be a 'common sense' understanding, but to understand the nature and role of the term 'policing' we need to engage in a deeper analysis of its function within a given society.

Indeed, there is a school of thought that suggests a prerequisite for social order is the need for a police organisation; yet Reiner further suggests that many societies have, in fact, existed without a formal police force of any kind. The 'police' are therefore not found in every society, but 'policing' may still be undertaken by a number of different processes and institutional arrangements. What we come to understand as the state-sanctioned police agency today is only one example of policing.

The idea of 'the police' is therefore a relatively modern concept, while 'policing' is an old one (Johnston, 1992). Prior to the 18th century, the term 'police' was used to explain the broad function of 'policing' – that is, the general regulation of the government, morals or economy of a city or country. The word 'police' is derived from the Greek word '*polis*' meaning 'city state'. 'Policing' thus referred to a socio-political function, instead of a formal legal one, that was exercised in any civil society, not just within the confines of the state. It was only in the mid-18th century that the word 'police' began to be used in its 'continental' sense in Great Britain, to refer to the specific functions of crime prevention and order maintenance. This idea is reinforced by Radzinowicz (1956), who states that by the middle of the 18th century there was already a growing realisation that the traditional arrangements for keeping the peace had become inadequate. However, it was a further 75 years before a radical break was effected and a modern police established with the Metropolitan Police Act

1829. Indeed, when the word 'police' was first introduced into England in the early part of the 18th century, it was regarded with the utmost suspicion, and was widely believed to be part of the sinister force that held France in its grip. In the early 1720s in England, the word was in fact almost unknown. However, by the time of John Fielding, the word 'police' began to gain currency, and Fielding began using it in the title of a pamphlet he wrote in 1758 (Fielding, cited in Radzinowicz [1956]). He subsequently used the word in other publications, and it gradually became used to define not just government policies – as it had in Fielding's original publication – but also the regulation of such policies. As the 18th century progressed, its use became more familiar and the term began to refer to themes more akin to its modern meaning, including the maintenance of good order and the prevention or detection of offences.

It is important to understand the differentiation between the terms 'police' and 'policing', especially as we enter a period of profound change for the police organisation. Indeed, Lister and Jones (2015) believe that the recognition of the conceptual and empirical decoupling of 'police' and 'policing' has generated a breadth of scholarly debate concerning how we might make sense of contemporary systems of crime control, regulation, social ordering and so on, as well as understanding the implication that arises for relations between state, market and civil society.

Defining a definition

While it would be easy to simply accept Waddington's (1999) answer to the question 'What is policing?' as being that which police officers do, it is in fact a far more complex role. We have seen that we need to separate out the term 'police' from the much broader term 'policing' in order to understand current changes in our society. However, in order to assist us in understanding and negotiating change in terms of policing, we need to consider a fully working definition of 'policing' as it relates all those involved in its application.

In truth, Waddington does consider a more serious definition when he concludes that policing is the authority of the state over the civil population and that this authority is based on the monopoly of legitimate coercion, which means the police will ask someone to do or not to do something and they will normally comply. If they do not comply, the police will force them to do so. This agrees with Klockars' (1985) earlier definition of the police organisation as being 'institutions or individuals given the general right to use coercive force by the state within the state's domestic territory' (Klockars, 1985, p 12).

In terms of the application of such a definition, the American sociologist Egon Bittner (1970, p 30) described such incidents as situations where 'something ought not to be happening and about which something ought to be done now'. The important word in this phrase is 'now', which indicates that all of these situations have the feature that they cannot wait for resolution. The crucial element in Bittner's discussion is therefore that of time. With the general right to use coercive force, the police are able to do something 'now', as the police are able to overcome resistance by use of their legal powers of coercion.

What is interesting about Bittner's idea is that the 'something' that is happening that needs attention remains undefined. So it may include many incidents that on the surface may not be seen as police business but that the police become involved in and resolve.

If 'police' is a term specific to a group of individuals charged with special crime and disorder reduction powers, then 'policing' is a much wider concept and involves many other agencies.

Crawford (2014) sees policing as the outcome of a constellation of actors, agencies and processes both within and beyond the police organisation. Policing therefore can be defined as the wider application of many agencies in order to support the functions of the state in reducing crime and disorder. It includes the work of educational bodies that attempt to prevent crime through the education of citizens away from this activity, as well as community cohesion activities that promote active citizenry and volunteerism. Private security companies and other agencies are also member of the wider 'constellation' of bodies that work to support the state. However, private security, according to Crawford, tends to be more instrumental than moral, in the sense that it is concerned more with loss prevention and risk reduction than with law enforcement and conviction of criminals. Nonetheless, both the activities of the police and of those involved in the wider process of policing are of course engaged with the idea of social control.

Social control as function

Traditionally, when one thinks of the role of the state with the visible idea of social control, one immediately thinks of the uniformed police officer. However, not all policing is carried out by the police, but involves a diverse range of agencies and organisations. The term social control is often used to indicate a form of organised reaction to deviant behaviour. This approach is in part based on the work of Stanley Cohen, who defined social control as being those 'organised responses to crime, delinquency and allied forms of deviant and/or socially problematic behaviour which are actually conceived of as such, whether in the reactive sense (after the putative act has taken place or the actor been identified) or in the proactive sense (to prevent the act)' (Cohen, 1985, p 3).

According to this definition, social control refers to the mechanisms used to regulate the conduct of people who are seen as deviant, criminal, worrying or troublesome in some way by others. Importantly for us, the ways in which different cultures understand and respond to different forms of problematic behaviour changes and alters. However, whatever the factors that combine to explain and deal with problematic behaviour are, the main objective is to control behaviour that is seen to be problematic or deviant in some way. Innes (2003) points out that although Cohen's definition may be restricting in its scope as it focuses on deviant acts, it is sufficiently flexible to allow for social control strategies to be implemented by state agencies or by employees of private corporations. Indeed, it could be argued that much work in this area has been overly concerned with the role of the state and legal institutions, ignoring the fact that state action (of which the police are one example) is perhaps only a small part of how social actions are controlled in everyday life. Reiner (2010) appears to concur with this idea that police cannot be seen as coterminous with social control but must be seen as a specific aspect of it. Policing does not encompass all activities directed at achieving social order; other agencies work towards achieving this goal as well.

Democratic policing

The influence of Peelian principles

When discussing modern policing, particularly in terms of the democratic policing model, one cannot ignore the fact that much has been written concerning the influence of Sir Robert Peel, who was Home Secretary in 1829. Countries such as the US claim to have introduced their ideas about the police and policing from the principles allegedly invoked by Peel (Peak and Glensor, 1996). It is he, along with the first two police commissioners for London, Sir Charles Rowan and Sir Richard Mayne, who are generally credited with the introduction of the first professional police forces in England and Wales from which the police of many other countries developed.

One concept in particular that is regularly referred to is Peel's principles of policing. This has recently become a topical issue again as the very nature of police and policing in England and Wales is changing; indeed, the fundamentals of community policing and the democratic style of policing are often cited as owing a great debt to Peel's ideas. Peel's principles are summarised in the box below.

Box 1.1: Peel's principles of policing

1. The basic mission of the police is to prevent crime.
2. The ability of the police to perform their duty is dependent upon public approval of police existence.
3 The police must secure the willing cooperation of the public in voluntarily .observing to keep the law.
4. The degree of public cooperation diminishes when physical force and compulsion is made in achieving police objectives.
5. Police should be impartial, friendly, and courteous and use humour and be ready to sacrifice themselves to protect and preserve life.
6. Physical force should be used only as necessary to secure observance of the law.
7. The police are the public and the public are the police.
8. The police should direct their actions towards this function and should not act as judge and jury.
9. The test of police efficiency is the absence of crime and disorder, not the visible evidence of police action in dealing with them.

Source: Adapted from Melville Lee (1901).

The general thrust of the principles concerns crime prevention and the concept of working with the community. Indeed, these principles are often quoted as being the foundation of the later community policing approach (Peak and Glensor 1996). However, despite extensive reference to these principles by many authors such as Melville Lee (1901) and Reith (1956), the fact is that only secondary sources exist for these ideas attributed to Peel; their exact origins remain shrouded in mystery. Indeed, Lentz and Chaire (2007), in their extensive examination of the literature surrounding the principles, go so far as to say they are largely the invention of 20th-century textbook authors and not directly attributable to the invention of the police in 1829, while Emsley (2014) suggests they have developed a mythical quality of their own.

Irrespective of this claim, the principles remain a fundamental plank within the discourse of modern policing and its future in a pluralised environment. Questions arise concerning whether or not these principles can be maintained within a new police paradigm, involving diverse agencies and a greater involvement of non-police personnel with a different form of accountability. Despite these questions, however, the principles themselves are commensurate with the idea we refer to as the democratic style of policing.

Democratic-style policing

The British police approach is widely associated with the idea of a democratic policing model (for example, see Independent Police Commission, 2013). Though contested, the democratic policing model is premised on several key assumptions that will be explored in more depth later. As Dunleavy and O'Leary (1987) point out, the concept of democracy is best understood through its Greek roots, with *demos* meaning 'the citizen body' and *cracy* meaning 'the rule of'. Therefore the great advantage of public policing in democratic countries is that it is accountable to every citizen through the mechanisms of representative government (Bayley and Shearing, 2005). This in turn means that the police have a legitimacy within communities, which makes the application of their duties much easier. Defining the idea of a democratic policing model can, however, be difficult (Manning, 2010). While the antithesis of democratic policing is the police state, democracy itself has many meanings and definitions; yet despite this diversity, there are certain important underlying themes and elements to the idea of democracy. These are consensus, freedom and equality, within which the concept of democratic policing needs to be situated. The following sections consider these underlying themes in greater detail and help us situate the policing process in a democratic society.

Consensus

All politically civilised societies owe their continuing existence to a consensus concerning the foundations of society (Berkley, 1969). Citizens agree on a common purpose, the procedures by which these purposes are to be effected and the institutions that are intended to preserve them. Without consensus, therefore, no democratic system would survive for long. Aligned to the concept of consensus is the idea that society allows policing by consent, which is a crucial concept for how we think about public policing in most Western societies. Countries such as the US, the UK and Canada have historically been sources of police expertise and training for developing countries, based on the premise that policing is supported by consensus and the consent of the public. By comparing police systems based on consent and consensus with alternative, state-centred, social-ordered systems, consent-based policing generally appears in a favourable light (Sklansky, 2008). This is not to suggest that everything in the democratic policing model is beyond criticism, of course, and the consent of some groups to being policed has sometimes been lacking or unsatisfactory (Goldsmith, 2001). One example is the policing of some minority ethnic groups in different countries. Nonetheless, the rhetoric of needing the consent of the people to be policed still appears to retain a certain value.

However, the idea of a model of policing based on near-full consent of the governed is now open to question. Broad social changes, as well as changes to police management, mean that there needs to be a reappraisal of the idea of consent-based policing. As Fukuyama (1999, 2005) suggests, there has been a rise in scepticism and distrust among citizens in developed societies towards institutions representing political authority and public service. This scepticism can also erode the confidence required to support the idea of legitimacy from the public that the police require. However, few would argue that this should lead to the end of the police.

Freedom and equality

Another vital element of democracy is 'freedom', and in particular the idea that individuals in society have the freedom to participate in politically motivated discussions and are able to hold government officials to account. Police do not meet citizens on an equal footing. Police are equipped with additional legal powers, both formal and informal, and they also carry weapons as the tools of their trade (Sklansky, 2008). However, no matter how efficient the police may be and no matter how careful they are to observe long-standing civil liberties, they will always have to fight against an undercurrent of opposition and criticism from some citizens, who are also the very people they are paid to serve and protect and to which, in the last analysis, they are responsible. In the UK in particular, the manifestation of the democratic police model can be seen in the approach commonly referred to as community policing.

Community policing

Neoliberal ideas of governance in general in the late 1980s and 1990s encompassed the attractive nostalgic idea that local police officers are best responsive to local communities (Reiner, 2010), a notion that has been assisted by a growing trend towards the devolution by the state of policing functions that were previously the responsibility of state-sponsored policing providers to individuals, groups and communities. Neoliberalism can be defined as follows:

> An approach to economic and social studies in which control of economic factors is shifted from the public sector to the private sector. Drawing upon principles of neo-classical economics, neo-liberalism suggests that governments reduce deficit spending, limit subsidies, reform tax laws to broaden the tax base, remove fixed exchange rates, open up markets to trade by limiting protectionism, privatise state-run businesses, allow private property and support de-regulation. (www.investopedia.com/terms/n/ neoliberalism.asp?layout=infini&v=4A&adtest=4A, accessed 17 March 2016)

This has also been referred to as the responsibilisation policy (Garland, 2001), whereby citizens and organisations are encouraged to start their own anti-crime measures and an entire preventative community infrastructure has grown up in addition to the police and the criminal justice system.

Community policing is a product of this approach with the intention that through community policing, communities can start to take ownership of identifying and solving their own crime and disorder problems. There is a link here to the government's ideas surrounding the concept of the Big Society, despite the fact that this idea is a more modern concept than that of community policing, and the use of volunteers is discussed later in this book. From a policing point of view, the concept expects individuals and community groups to increasingly assume responsibility for dealing with crime and disorder within their communities.

Much has been written about exactly what constitutes community policing (see Trojanowicz and Bucqueroux, 1990; Rogers, 2012; and Palmiotto, 2013, for example). However, one useful understanding of community policing is provided by Friedman (1992), which builds upon Trojanowicz's earlier work (Trojanowicz, 1983). In essence, community policing receives its mandate for existence from community support and from police professionalism. Its broad function is the provision of services in a decentralised environment that features intimate, informal and formal relationships with the public. Supporting the idea are principles developed as a result of experiments carried out by the Michigan State University emanating from the Flint Foot Patrol Experiment, which examined the daily interactions between police officers and community and the negotiation involved in that process (Trojanowicz 1983). In brief, these principles are as follows:

- community policing is a philosophy and a strategy;
- it requires implementation by all personnel;
- it requires a new type of police officer;
- it requires the police to work closely with volunteers;
- it introduces a different kind of relationship between police officers and citizens;
- it adds a proactive dimension to police work;
- it aims to protect the most vulnerable in society;
- it seeks to balance human skills with technological innovations.

One of the greatest strengths of community policing, however, is that it assists in supporting the legitimacy for the police. This is considered vital for community and police to work together to deal with crime and other types of disorder. Underpinning the community policing approach is the strong idea of community involvement. This is commonly referred to as community engagement.

Community engagement

Community engagement represents another central (albeit contested) concept within contemporary and mainstream policing discourses. Myhill (2006, p iv) defined community engagement as:

> [...] the process of enabling the participation of citizens and communities in policing at their chosen level, ranging from providing information and reassurance, to empowering them to identify and implement solutions to local problems and influence strategic priorities and decisions.

Although it clearly carries appeal for both police and community, the process of community engagement is rarely straightforward in practice. Indeed, Matrix (2007, cited in Lloyd and Foster, 2009) notes that community engagement represents a complex process for police services in so-called democratic societies. Lloyd and Foster, in a typology of 'engagers and non-engagers', distinguish between those more and less 'active' and socially networked citizens who enjoy different relationships with the police, where offending/non-offending and 'community anchor' status are key mediating features. Myhill (2006) also highlights the challenges involved (from the police perspective) of engaging more deeply and widely with the community with the aim of enhanced partnership working. These centre on:

- sustaining commitment;
- power-sharing issues;
- resolving tensions and conflicts within police performance measurement systems;
- organisational training and culture change;
- mainstreaming community engagement;
- development of community trust, confidence and capacities; and
- safeguarding the role of the community beat officer.

Community engagement, of course, helps to sustain a most important facet of policing in a democratic society – that of police legitimacy.

Police legitimacy

In any democratic policing model, the acceptance of police legitimacy is paramount if the police and community are to work together (Tyler and Huo, 2002). Police legitimacy has been described as the right to rule and the recognition by the ruled of that right. Therefore, despite the fact that police organisations are given the right to rule by the state or government, legitimacy only exists when it is perceived by the public. Research suggests that legitimacy traditionally captures the degree to which citizens have trust and confidence in authorities and, importantly, are willing to obey the directives of authorities such as the police (Hough et al, 2010). Additionally, the moral alignment of police and the public, through shared similar values for example, has been seen to be an additional and important element of police legitimacy. Further research also suggests that there are two key elements that support legitimacy (Tyler, 2003). The first is the way people perceive police performance. This refers to how well the police do their job, as police will not achieve the legitimacy they need if they lack the ability to be successful in carrying out their core functions of tackling crime and disorder. The second is what has been termed 'procedural justice', which broadly refers to the quality of police treatment and the quality of police decision making. There are several key elements of procedural justice, including dignity and respect, trustworthy motives, neutrality and voice. When police treat people with respect, demonstrate trustworthiness, are neutral in their decision making and provide people with an opportunity to participate in the process and air concerns before decisions are made, people are more likely to believe police are being procedurally just. It is the widespread use of procedural justice that is one of the most effective ways to promote police legitimacy. Procedural justice is important therefore for fundamental reasons, but there are other factors that justify its importance. The first is that people tend to comply with the law when the police are not around if procedural justice is used; thus, compliance with the law is not purely explained solely by the threat of punishment or the use of coercive power. Additionally, utilising this approach will make the police more effective in their work of controlling crime and disorder as they will be able to ensure valuable assistance from the general public, including those considered as the most vulnerable in society. Communities can help the police become more efficient in their day-to-day activities of crime control and prevention work, and this of course increases confidence in the police, and supports and even increases the idea of police legitimacy. The danger, of course, is that in times of austerity and budgetary reductions, this aspect of police– community interaction suffers. One approach to maintaining police–community interaction, it is argued, is the introduction and cultivation of the concept of 'expert citizens'. Expert citizens are seen as a key means to reduce the burden of demand on the police by using them in preventing crime, defending property and improving the resilience of their communities. Encouraging and enabling citizens to become 'expert', not only through taking steps to keep their person and property safe, but also through all of their interactions with the police service, will, it is argued, enable the police to meet the challenges of the future (Fraser et al, 2014).

The police in England and Wales today

The effective allocation of finite resources needs to reflect not just economics, but a clear strategy of what the police should be doing. In 2012, Her Majesty's Inspectorate of Constabulary (HMIC) examined demand on the police and raised the issue of the 'absence of clarity around a single mission for policing' (HMIC, 2012a, p 6). The purpose of policing has shifted with successive governments. Conservative White Papers in the 1990s believed it was 'to catch criminals'; in 1997, Labour defined the police role as being 'to support a just and tolerant society;' in 2011, Theresa May stated she needed the police 'to be the tough, no-nonsense crime-fighters they signed up to become' (May,

2011). Messages that reinforce the police as crime fighters, particularly during times of austerity, do little to support the role of neighbourhood policing teams, which were not merely introduced to reduce crime (Skogan, 2006a). The aims of neighbourhood policing are broader, encompassing community engagement, fear reduction and tackling low-level disorder and antisocial behaviour. Neighbourhood policing teams also provide a social service, such as safeguarding or transporting people with mental ill health, tracking down missing persons, or diffusing local tensions or conflicts, often through means other than law enforcement. These are all held to be core areas of policing (Reiner, 2013). The degree to which the police undertake activities that have little to do with crime fighting is no better illustrated than by the Manchester Twitter experiment. Based on an analysis of the 3,200 calls they received over a 24-hour period, all of which were tweeted using the popular social media site, Greater Manchester Police estimated that the majority of these calls had little or nothing to do with crime.

Millie (2012) refers to this as the 'policification of social work'. Others describe it as 'mission drift'. The 'can-do' culture of policing has led police leaders to take on tasks wherever there is a service gap (Gibbs and Greenhalgh, 2014).

Having said this, neighbourhood policing teams clearly do carry out activities that contribute to crime reduction, as illustrated by the idea of the use of hot spotting, a technique that focuses on a small geographic area using intelligence and information that guides police resources to where they are needed. Even the model of reassurance policing, which concentrates on signal crimes within a community (Innes, 2004 and discussed later), includes a crime reduction element, although the emphasis is on reassuring the public that the police are present and will intervene if required. The combination of 'mission drift', cuts in police budgets and political demands to fight crime places the police service in a difficult and potentially precarious position. The main challenge is to pull back from functions without losing public confidence. With this in mind, it is worth looking at the public's top ten priorities for policing, which is taken from Louise Casey's review, *Engaging Communities in Fighting Crime* (2008).

The top ten policing approaches the public said they want to see are:

- **A service that takes action** – responsive, approachable, coming out quickly when called to incidents, acting on, following up and feeding back on progress to members of the public when they report crime and anti-social behaviour.

- **A visible, uniformed police presence**, with police freed up from unnecessary red tape and health and safety restrictions, fewer constables and PCSOs taken off patrols to perform 'administrative' tasks, and there when needed, not just a nine-to-five service.
- **PCSOs who are clearly distinguishable as part of the police service**, with uniforms, equipment and powers that match their role in patrolling communities, supporting local police and tackling anti-social behaviour.
- **Named contacts** and clear information about who is responsible for what locally, and how to contact them in both emergency and non-emergency situations.
- **Face-to-face access** at a police station, a surgery or a street meeting.
- **Continuity in the local policing team**, with officers and PCSOs serving a minimum of two years in the neighbourhood so that they get to know areas and communities well and gain communities' respect and trust.
- **A better service for victims** of crime, especially repeat victims, returning regularly to check they are alright and to help minimise further victimisation.
- **Sensitivity over reporting** crime and giving evidence, protecting anonymity.
- **Good engagement with the community** to identify their priorities for action and to give feedback on action and outcomes on cases of greatest community concern.
- **Clear leadership from the police on crime** – with the backing of other organisations like the local council, prosecutors, the courts and probation services.

Clearly, neighbourhood policing, arguably the most threatened section of the police service, has an important role to play in delivering many of these priorities, from visibility and accessibility to effective engagement with communities and tackling antisocial behaviour. In fact, as recommended by the Independent Police Commission (2013) report by Lord Stevens, the Casey review states that the government should ensure the provision of a local police commitment in every neighbourhood, based on the 9 Peel principles outlined earlier. Through positive engagement, for example, neighbourhood policing teams can encourage people to come forward with information to help keep their own neighbourhood safe. The public want face-to-face contact with officers and police community support officers (PCSOs) they know and feel able to trust. In HMIC's all-force comparison public survey, when asked which forms of communication would make them feel safer in their local area, around half of respondents identified face-to-face interaction with a police officer or PCSO on patrol (HMIC, 2013). By being a consistent and familiar presence in communities, neighbourhood policing teams can build confidence and trust in the police and consequently foster greater compliance with the law (Sunshine and Tyler, 2003). Neighbourhood policing officers are also well placed to identify problems – most of which are directly related to crime – at an early stage, such as poor parenting, substance misuse or mental ill health (Home Office, 2010a). In many respects, neighbourhood policing is core business, as the Independent Police Commission report by Lord Stevens claims:

> Neighbourhood policing is not simply a desirable option that can be shaved in order to affect cost savings. Rather, it is the key building block of effective and legitimate policing and vital in responding to public expectations and building and sustaining confidence. This in turn is likely to improve and increase the public's engagement with the police in terms of giving them information and being willing to act as witnesses, essential ingredients if the police are to do more with less. (Independent Police Commission, 2013, p 15)

The latest figures available for police officer numbers (2015) show the total number of police officers in England and Wales as being 126,818. This is illustrated in Table 1.1.

The data illustrates that the police officer workforce is predominantly male, with the total number of female officers accounting for just over 28% of the total workforce. The total number of constables and sergeants is shown as being 118,102 and it is they, along with PCSOs and special constables who undertake the day-to-day activities normally associated with the public police, as well as providing numbers for specialised roles such as CID and family support. They also provide staff for central service in national policing agencies and functions.

It is worth noting the trend in the reduction of constables over time. Table 1.2 illustrates this trend.

As can be seen, the general trend in reduction of front-line constables is important to acknowledge and reflects government philosophy and economic conditions.

Table 1.1: Total number of police officers by rank in England and Wales, March 2015

Rank	Male	Female	Total	% Male	% Female
Chief officers	158	43	201	78.6	21.4
Chief superintendent	265	72	337	78.7	21.3
Superintendent	663	157	820	80.8	19.2
Chief inspector	1,283	374	1,657	77.4	22.6
Inspector	4,550	1,152	5,701	79.8	20.2
Sergeant	15,123	4,024	19,148	79.0	21.0
Constable	69,039	29,915	98,954	69.8	30.2
All ranks	91,081	35,738	126,818	71.8	28.2

Source: Home Office (2015).

Table 1.2: Total number of police constables in England and Wales by year

Year (as at 31 March)	Total police constables
2003	104,380
2004	109,715
2005	110,392
2006	109,851
2007	109,400
2008	108,884
2009	110,080
2010	109,669
2011	106,609
2012	102,934
2013	99,619
2014	99,107
2015	98,954

Source: Home Office (2015).

In terms of the make-up of the whole police workforce, Figure 1.1 illustrates how many staff other than police officers are currently involved in the delivery of, and support for, the public police.

Figure 1.1: Constituents of total police workforce as of March 2015

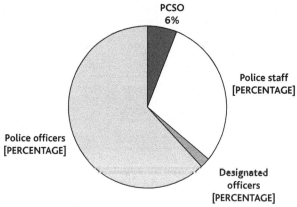

Source: Home Office (2015)

Police officers make up by far the majority of staff working in the police organisation, but it is anticipated that the number of police officers making up the total workforce will probably decrease over the next five years or so. However, this data does not include such voluntary occupations as special constables, other police volunteers or those involved in security or private forms of policing.

Conclusion

It is clear that the ideas of 'police' and 'policing' are complex but can be distinguished from one another in form and definition. We have become used to a coterminous application and understanding of these concepts, with one implying the same as the other in terms of definition. However, by separating the concepts, we can begin to understand the changing landscape of the provision of policing services in England and Wales and how this will be influenced.

The process of change has already begun. When one examines the role of the police as it stands today and considers the reduction in the number of front-line police officers, a trend that will inevitably continue, we can begin to understand some of the challenges that lie ahead, especially at a local level. It is therefore vital that we understand where we are now in terms of our policing provision to appreciate the scale, nature and impact of the changes ahead. Questions will, of course, arise regarding efficiency, costs and accountability in the new world of plural policing. It is this idea of plural policing that we focus on in the next chapter.

Further reading

Berkley, G. E. (1969) *The Democratic Policeman*, Boston, MA: Beacon Press.

Berry, J. (2007) 'Officer numbers could be slashed', available at www.policemag.co.uk/Archive/2006/0606/0606.pdf (accessed 26 November 2015).

Bittner, E. (1970) 'Florence Nightingale in pursuit of Willie Sutton: a theory of the police', in E. Bittner (ed) *The Functions of the Police in Modern Society*, Cambridge, MA: Oelgeschlager, Gunn and Hain Publishers.

Casey, L. (2008) *Engaging communities in fighting crime*, London: Cabinet Office.

Cohen, S. (1985) *Visions of Social Control*, Cambridge: Polity Press.

College of Policing (2015a) 'Estimating demand on the police service', available at www.college.police.uk/News/College-news/Documents/Demand%20Report%2023_1_15_noBleed.pdf (accessed November 2015).

Dunleavy, P. and O'Leary, B. (1987) *Theories of the State: The Politics of Liberal Democracy*, London: Macmillan.

Friedman, R. (1992) *Community Policing: Comparative Perspectives and Prospects*, New York, NY: Prentice Hall.

Halpern, D. (2007) *Social Capital*, Cambridge: Polity Press.

Hough, M., Jackson, J., Bradford, B., Myhill, A. and Quinton, P. (2010) 'Procedural justice, trust and institutional legitimacy', *Oxford Journal of Policing*, vol 4, no 3, pp 1-8.

Jones, T. (2008) 'The accountability of policing', in T. Newburn (ed) *The Handbook of Policing*, Cullompton: Willan.

Klockars, C. (1985) *The Idea of Police*, Beverley Hills, CA: Sage Publications.

Palmiotto, M.J. (2013) *Community Policing: A Police Citizen Partnership*, Abingdon: Routledge.

Reiner, R. (2010) *The Politics of the Police* (4th edn), Oxford: Oxford University Press.

TWO

Discussing plural policing

Introduction

We saw in the previous chapter how the terms 'police' and 'policing' are contested and have each developed a different meaning from their original inception. This illustrates the complexity of trying to define such ideas as 'police' and 'policing': they mean different things to different people at different times. It is much the same when discussing the idea of plural policing. Plural policing can be described as a new way of looking at policing that may now have moved away from a police-centric view of the world (Crawford, 2008), and includes a new way of viewing the social system that surrounds policing itself. In particular, this involves the growth of the non-public sector policing provision of policing activities. As we saw in Chapter One, when discussing exactly what is meant by policing, there has been a focus on policing purely from the view of the uniformed services provided by the public police organisation. However, we need to move away from the idea that 'policing' is associated purely with the work of the uniformed public police alone. This is an important point that needs to be reinforced, but to understand the current and ongoing trend for plural policing we need to situate the present state (and future) of police activity in an historical context.

Recent historical context

The current structure of 43 police forces in England and Wales reflects in part the historical fear of a national police force. The historical context of this concern can be found in the period before the introduction of the Metropolitan Police Act 1829, with the popular fear that a national police could easily become puppets of the government, which could lead to anarchy and direct political control. People pointed to examples of the misuse of the police in European countries, particularly Revolutionary France, to support this argument; hence the fragmentation of British police forces, with the accent on so-called 'local accountability'. However, as Jones (2008) points out, the general trend in recent times has been one of greater centralised control of local policing, with the Home Office exerting more influence and the establishment of national policing bodies such as the Serious Organised Crime Agency (now the National Crime Agency). Other national bodies include Her Majesty's Inspectorate of Constabulary (HMIC), the Audit Commission and the Police Standards Unit among others, which have been important actors in the national governance of policing in England and Wales (Jones and Van Sluis, 2009).

While this focus on centralised control has been a feature of recent Labour governments, the coalition and Tory administrations since 2010 seem to have invoked looser central control, with the introduction of a system of elected Police and Crime Commissioners (PCCs) in November 2012 under the auspices of the Police and Social Responsibility Act (Home Office, 2011) and the end of ring-fenced funding for community policing. The introduction of the PCC role, with the revised funding arrangements for that post meaning that incumbents can decide how to spend their budgets, introduces the possibility for further pluralisation of policing services.

Until recently, governments in the UK have sought to expand police numbers until by 2010 the number of police officers in England and Wales stood at 141,000. However, since that time large expenditure cuts have meant that 20 per cent of funding for police has been removed. In the current climate of austerity, this economic reduction is likely to continue. HMIC (2014) has projected that there will be 16,300 fewer police officers in England and Wales in the near future. It is therefore understandable that an increased interest in a pluralised policing approach would appear to be linked with the idea of reduced funding for policing.

However, even during the times when police numbers were being increased, there was evidence to suggest that pluralisation of policing was being undertaken, albeit within the police organisation itself. The most obvious example is the introduction of police community support officers (PCSOs) (discussed in more depth in Chapter Five). Established by section 38 of the Police Reform Act 2002, these 'civilian' or unsworn officers are directed and controlled by the chief constable. They undergo much less rigorous training and have fewer legal powers than sworn officers. Because they are cheaper to employ than regular officers, they are sometimes viewed as being the police's answer to competing with other (non-police) providers for local markets for patrol (Blair, 2003). Even before the introduction of PCSOs, however, the widening of police provision was contained within the Crime and Disorder Act 1998 (Home Office, 1998), which saw the formalisation of partnership working, and the introduction many other agencies, such as local authorities and education and health providers, being involved in crime reduction work.

In an interesting approach, Zedner (2006) suggests that the recent developments in policing are typical of an era that pre-dates the police themselves. She examines the historical aspect of crime control, and comes to the conclusion that the apparent monopoly of policing by the public police can be seen as an historical blip in the long-term pattern of multiple police providers and markets in security. The extent and import of changes in contemporary crime control are therefore hotly contested. By setting these changes in historical perspective, Zedner challenges claims that we are entering a new era in policing.

Defining plural policing

As Ian Loader (2000) points out, we have seen a shift from 'police' to 'policing' and this has resulted in the recent modification of the work of the state, both as a sole provider and as a broader, more diverse network of power. Loader provides four distinct categories of policing, namely:

- private forms of policing secured through government;
- transnational forms of policing that are above government;
- the market in policing and security beyond government;
- policing activities engaged in by citizens themselves, considered to be below government.

This is a world of plural, networked policing. Consequently, issues attached to an older, single-style delivery of policing, such as legitimacy, effectiveness, equity and human rights, now present themselves with regard to plural policing.

Prenzler (2013), writing about the situation in Australia, concurs, pointing to the fact that the time of governments being viewed as the natural monopoly of many basic services, including health, education and policing, may be at an end.

Historically, of course, the role of the state as the sole provider of services, particularly policing, is not a consistent one. Johnston (1992) points to the fact that the field of private security history shows that private and other forms of non-police security have tended to dominate community business and individual forms of protection in the face of a common situation of absent or inadequate state provision.

For Crawford and colleagues (2005), the term 'plural policing' is utilised for the following reasons:

- It recognises the plurality of policing powers and personnel, and acknowledges the existence of a mixed economy.
- It breaks free from the unhelpful dichotomy between 'public' and 'private' police, recognising that sometimes public police serve private and parochial interests and police private spaces or privately owned spaces that have become public in character.
- It does not prioritise the role of any particular provider.

Wakefield (2009) believes that plural policing is the expanding role of non-police service providers in policing, and the variety of different public, private and voluntary bodies now engaged in the activity. Plural policing therefore refers to the patchwork of policing provision and authorisation which involves a mix of the police, municipal auxiliaries, commercial security and the activities of the citizens. This replaces the idea of the police being the sole proprietors of, or having a monopoly over, public security provision.

The term 'pluralisation' itself appears to emanate from the early work of Shearing and Stenning (1981; 1983), where they observed a change in the way formal social control was taking place, particularly in the increasing use of private security and an increase in different agencies delivering policing activities. Bayley and Shearing (1996) have argued that in modern democratic countries a watershed has been reached in terms of crime control and law enforcement, and that in the future people will view this time as one when an old system of policing ended and another took over.

It appears that to some extent pluralised policing has already gained a substantial foothold in policing in this country through recent innovations such as neighbourhood policing teams. It is, of course, tempting to assume that plural policing is limited to the UK. However, this is far from the truth and a study of the introduction of plural policing in other European countries compared with the situation in the UK is a fruitful one. Even allowing for the different social and political make-up of these countries, lessons may be learned from their experiences.

Plural policing in different countries

Terpstra and Van Stokkom (2015) and Terpstra and colleagues (2013) provide some useful information when considering the plural policing idea in other countries. They quite rightly point out that other agencies, both public and private, are now undertaking tasks that until quite recently were considered to be the tasks of the police alone, such as patrolling public spaces and the enforcement of social order. There now exist all kinds of non-police guards, patrollers, wardens and officers working in the public space under the gaze of the public. Consequently, it is useful to appreciate and understand how the pluralisation of policing in other countries is being undertaken, as it may be of relevance to our own context. Of course, policing does not occur in a vacuum and while the UK has been subject to a neoliberal agenda in recent years, this may not be the case for some other countries. Similar developments may have drastically different meanings in other social and cultural contexts, but may provide opportunities for learning and experience.

Austria

Austria has an entrenched legalistic culture with a strong political consensus that only the state should be responsible for policing and security matters. Consequently, its plural policing facilities are on a modest scale, with some local provision of two types of 'non-police' policing emerging since 2007. Between 15 and 20 municipal authorities have created local organisations responsible for surveillance and some enforcement for minor infractions in public spaces. The reason for this development lies in the fact that over the past two decades the police have become focused on national issues and fighting crime, with to the detriment of local community-style policing. Municipalities and cities have tried to counter this movement by establishing local organisations, some of which hire private security guards, to work in public spaces in order to provide a visible uniformed presence. However, there is a problem with this approach in that these security guards have no special powers, and while their numbers appear to be increasing, there is no special legislation in place to regulate their activity. Consequently, the presence of armed security guards on the street in Austria is not unusual, and the regulation of some 'non-police' policing appears to be fairly poor.

Belgium

Belgium has introduced different forms of policing since the 1990s in response to dissatisfaction with poor management of petty crime and social disorder. For example, the government has introduced job creation schemes for surveillance guards and community guards working in public areas. Further legislation was introduced in 2007 to give municipal authorities more power to manage petty crime and other low-level misdemeanours. As a consequence, the role of 'community guard reporter' was established, with incumbents entitled to report certain offences, with perpetrators receiving a fine or entering community service. However, the implementation of this approach appears to be fragmented across the country. That said, the public police are legally obliged to cooperate with the guards but not supervise them, the latter being responsibility of the municipal authorities. Private security in Belgium plays only a limited role in the public space, with the current consensus that surveillance (patrol) and enforcement in public spaces should only be performed by state institutions. Consequently, the debate regarding the use of private security for public policing has not really occurred in Belgium to date.

The Netherlands

The Netherlands appears to have a longer history of pluralised policing than most countries in Europe. City guards, or *Stadswachten*, were introduced mainly in city centres around 1989 with the task of patrolling public spaces, based not only on security for the public but as part of a job creation scheme for the long-term unemployed (Hauber et al, 1996). However, since the mid-2000s these guards have been employed by new and larger municipal departments of city surveillance or local enforcement agencies. Some local governments now appoint special investigative officers (SIOs) who patrol public spaces and who also have limited powers to deal with low-level social disorder. It would appear that around 14 per cent of municipal governments in the Netherlands also contract for special occasions employees of private security firms as wardens or SIOs for working in public areas. The main reason apparently is the flexibility it allows the municipalities, which can contract and pay for individuals when there is a clear need for their services.

In the Netherlands, the police have formal responsibility for the daily or operational coordination of these wardens. However, it is the municipal authorities who are responsible for policy, budgets and so on, which causes some problems in the implementation of warden schemes. Such problems include poor exchange of information and poor direction in terms of leadership from the police organisation, leading to difficult relationships between the police and the municipal authorities.

Private security guards are often used as wardens in semi-public places such as business parks and malls, and at large scale events (Van Steden and Sarre, 2007), while a small number are contracted by private agencies to work in the public area, for example in neighbourhoods where residents have high incomes and can afford to pay for private patrolling.

Consequently, in the Netherlands, there is a complex yet fragmented public and private provision of surveillance and enforcement officers working in public places. In general, the rise of the pluralised approach is rooted in the fact that the public police have been gradually withdrawing since the 1990s, both from rural areas and from basic street patrolling duties, with less attention being paid to high visibility police work.

Germany

The federal political system in Germany lends itself to a strong tradition of local self-government, and this affects the powers and responsibilities of the police. The police have responsibility for different aspects of law enforcement, while local authorities have their own responsibilities for public safety and public order (Frevel, 2015). Consequently, the evolution of plural policing has not been as prevalent as in other countries such as the UK, even if the concept of neoliberalism can be seen elsewhere in the political system.

During the early 1990s, there appeared to be a reduction in the sense of community safety and wellbeing. This, coupled with economic problems and altered perceptions of crime and risks, led to some reforms and new interpretations of police duties. In addition, according to Frevel (2015), the rise of the security market, including home security, led to an increase in this type of provision, which in turn pushed forward the idea of plural policing.

In the main, municipal authorities deal with such as issues as public order and safety, with specialised departments that employ occasionally uniformed staff who are involved in surveillance patrols and some enforcement. These city warden-type staff members are not allowed to use coercive force, but can call the police if the situation demands it. Police interaction with private security companies has tended to revolve around the traditional private security fields of patrols within private premises, building security and so on. However, there appears to be a growing trend of visible uniformed security personnel in semi-public and public spaces.

Despite recent changes in some areas of policing public space, Germany still primarily conforms to what Loader (2000) refers to as 'policing by government'. The police are a relatively well-regarded organisation in Germany and there have been some reservations regarding private security firms that do not have such public support. The consequence is that Germany still favours a lower grade of privatisation in the field of safety and security in terms of pluralised policing functions.

Conclusions from other countries

Having briefly considered some countries' experiences of pluralised policing, we can discern that most of these countries have seen an increase in the use of non-police providers of policing to a greater or lesser extent. The reasons for this seem to point to the police's failure to meet the expectation that they will be present in public spaces through surveillance patrols. This may be because of similar social and economic circumstances in each country, including the expansion of the night-time economy, raised expectations of security and the rise of national and international threats to name but a few examples.

Therefore what appears to have occurred is a shortage of resources to focus on so-called 'petty crime' and low-level disorder, which in turn has had a negative impact on community feelings of safety and security. Consequently, the regular or public police have focused on 'core tasks or functions' such as 'fighting crime' and dealing with the ever-increasing complexity and globalisation of the crime picture. The main negative impact of this has been seen and felt at the local level, where it is believed it affects people's trust and support for the police (Innes, 2014). As a result, local solutions to this problem appear to be the main drivers for newer kinds of uniformed 'police', such as city guards, wardens or private security guards, who operate alongside the regular or public police. These roles are mainly controlled and supported by municipal authorities and, while these guards operate alongside regular police, they are not managed or dominated by them. As Terpstra and colleagues (2013) point out, what we see in continental European countries is the increasing importance of local authorities being responsible for local safety policies.

Despite what appear to be some commonalties within the introduction of pluralised policing in these countries, there are of course some differences in the way the non-police personnel operate. For example, some countries have a strict legal agreement regarding the way in which each group operates, with some close relationships between police and non-police personnel. On the other hand, there can be some distance between police and security guards who carry out enforcement duties in public. The countries also differ in terms of the extent to which the private police carry out their function. For example, Belgium currently has no private guards who have patrol and enforcement tasks in public, because the general consensus is that these tasks should remain in public hands. In contrast, local authorities in the Netherlands can contract private security guards that may have some formal legal powers, while private security officers can be contracted by residents to provide security patrols.

Plural policing as vertical policing

Plural policing is commonly thought of as being lateral in content; that is, team workers working at the same level of interaction and responsibility, perhaps commonly seen through the neighbourhood policing team approach, where information is shared laterally between different agencies in an attempt to problem solve at a local community level. However, another way of viewing plural policing is through the vertical model. Innes (2003) points out that one of the defining characteristics of late modern forms of social control is that whereas previously different sites and sources of social control were fairly distinct and discrete, increasingly the boundaries between them are being blurred. For example, in terms of welfare provision, the implementation and delivery of social control is based on overlapping and interspersed strategies, technologies and personnel. These connections are vertical in that individuals, communities and a variety of public agencies have all been enlisted into a large number of state-sponsored programmes designed to tackle crime.

The neighbourhood policing team approach discussed later in this work is a good example of this vertical concept. Several different groups of people come together with a common aim, which is generally concerned with the reduction or prevention of crime and disorder in a defined geographical area. Here, what we see are different levels of organisations providing a broad policing function, interlocking and interlinking to provide a broader approach to policing in general or to something quite specific. This approach relies on the gathering and utilisation of good community and criminal intelligence, which is fed upwards and downwards and may be visualised in Figure 2.1.

Different types of police and policing agencies are engaged in the process of gathering and analysing intelligence, which flows in both directions and is an example of the vertical approach to plural policing. The use of information and intelligence therefore can be a useful by-product of pluralised policing, and worthy of further consideration.

Figure 2.1: Levels of engagement for intelligence use

International level	→	Tackle global threats including cyber terrorism
National level	→	Tackle srious national crime and provide central support for forces
Individual force level	→	Combating serious and specialist crime
Police basic command level	→	Respond to local area crime such as burglary etc
Neighbourhood level	→	Reduce fear of drime, tackle neighbourhood problems

Information and intelligence flows in both directions

Source: Adapted from Home Office (2006)

Information and intelligence

Community and criminal intelligence are of great importance if the multiple and pluralised police services available to the police manager are to be directed effectively. This would be greatly enhanced by the ability of the public to have direct access in many cases to the providers, who can then react more quickly to the community's needs.

Consultation with the community at this level, through formal structures such as regular meetings with representatives from the community and surgeries for the public to attend and share their concerns, coupled with sophisticated community intelligence available to the police, will be effective tools in the drive to maintain order. It is envisaged (John and Maguire, 2004) that the link between this model and the National Intelligence Model will be forged through the normal tasking and intelligence briefing groups held within every BCU (Basic Command Unit).

In the new pluralised world of policing, the drive for operational intelligence and information should be a priority. The question arises regarding how such information should be stored and managed in policing work where several public and private agencies come together to provide a service. The sharing of information has, for many years, been problematic for community safety partnerships, for example, despite there being adequate provision for such work specified within the Crime and Disorder Act 1998 (Home Office, 1998). While the gathering, storage and management of information and intelligence may become problematic for pluralised policing activities, the approach may also suffer from problems of accountability or lack of it.

Accountability in a pluralised policing environment

An apparently contentious area when discussing a pluralised form of policing is that of accountability. Police provision is no longer monopolised by the public police, that is, the police entrusted by government with a monopoly on the use of state-sanctioned force (Klockars, 1985). Policing is now widely offered by institutions other than the state, most importantly by private companies on a commercial basis and by communities on a volunteer basis. The great advantage of public policing in democratic countries is that it is *accountable* to every citizen through the mechanisms of representative government. This is not the case for commercial private policing organisations, which are accountable – ultimately – to their shareholders. This form of accountability is, of course, problematic and is discussed in more depth in Chapter Three.

Several major works have historically described and analysed democratic accountability of policing and its importance. Established scholars such as Bittner (1980), Sklansky (2008) and Punch (2011) have all contributed to the notion that democratic policing cannot survive without accountability. In support of these seminal writers, one of the most important documents regarding democratic accountable policing in Europe is the 2008 publication by the Organisation for Security and Cooperation Europe (OSCE, 2008). This word reinforces the key principles of democratic policing, in particular police accountability and transparency. Here, democratic policing requires that the police be and consider themselves to be accountable to:

- the citizens;
- their representatives;
- the state; and
- the law.

Public police activities, therefore, ranging from behaviour and attitude, strategies for police operations, appointment procedures and even budget management, must be open to scrutiny by a variety of supervisory institutions. Furthermore, if a central feature of democratic policing is the *consent* of the people, prerequisites for gaining public support should be 'providing transparency in police operations and (ensuring) mutual understanding with the public the police serve and protect' (OSCE, 2008, p 13). The recent introduction of Police and Crime Commissioners in England and Wales is considered partly to be a bridge between communities and the police as a mechanism to strengthen police accountability to the public (Rogers and Gravelle, 2012).

Police accountability requires police officers and the institutions to which they belong to explain, justify and answer for their conduct. Individual police officers are obliged to account internally to their supervisors and to an internal investigation unit, and, in democracies, to external independent accountability institutions such as the Independent Police Complaints Commission (IPCC) in the UK.

At a political level, police agencies commonly answer to a senior member of government such as a police minister. This political structure of accountability is influenced by the particular political system in the state. For example, a totalitarian state would regard the police as a 'tool' of the government. In democratic societies, the police are required to:

- adhere to the law;
- abide by due process when enforcing the law; and
- protect citizens' rights, both civil and political, within the power laid down by legislation.

Ultimately, despite the perceived laborious route involved in getting change introduced in the democratic political model, accountability to people does occur through their elected representation.

What has been witnessed in many countries in the past decade or so has been a rise in external civilian regulatory bodies that have slowly become an acceptable feature of police accountability, for example the use of lay visitors in the UK.

The role of external civilian regulatory bodies is to monitor, review and/or investigate alleged corruption and misconduct. Given that police accountability in the UK is, in the main, one of the roles of local government, this type of approach would seem to fit adequately into any future accountability process.

To be effective, the 'policing by consent' model requires the community to trust its police, and that trust is dependent on police behaviour according to constitutional and legal processes established by the people through a freely elected representative parliament. The public sector management techniques that have been introduced in various Acts of Parliament and Home Office circulars since the 1980s/1990s have resulted in improvements in budgetary, financial and organisational matters, while the media reporting of police-related scandals has kept police accountability firmly on the political agenda.

There is, of course, one perceived complication when discussing police accountability, and that is the idea of constabulary or operational independence. This highlights the difference between the government's right to formulate policing policy and state interference with operational policing decisions, including the exercise of policing powers. In other words, elected politicians can produce policy relating to what needs to be done by the police, but the way in which these policies are implemented is decided by chief police officers.

Consequently 'operational independence' requires the police:

- to have a high degree of professionalism and independence from political influences;
- to act in conformity with the law and established practice;
- to operate on the basis of public consent as evidenced by levels of public confidence;
- to take responsibility for their decisions and operations, accepting liability when required and to exhibit full transparency in decisions and openness to external scrutiny.

This is particularly important in terms of helping the police achieve full public confidence as this is the key to effective policing, whereby police functions are carried out on the basis of legitimacy rather than force.

As Jones (2008) rightly points out, the provision of pluralised policing, which includes both public and private bodies, introduces challenges for those responsible for ensuring that policing is under the control and influence of the democratic policing model. He points to four main areas of concern, namely:

- The range of providers of policing activities raises the question of identifying who these providers are and making sure their activities are visible and transparent.
- The complex provision of different agencies duplicating their efforts may influence the effectiveness of the approach.
- Specific sections or disadvantaged groups may be over- or under-policed if the plural policing approach is not delivered in an equal fashion.

- If policing provision is fragmented, it is more difficult for police services to be responsive to community needs and values.

Given the problems highlighted above, the challenge is, of course, to institute an accountability and governance strategy that deals with the full approach to pluralised policing. This strategy may be similar to the policing board index introduced in Northern Ireland as a result of the Patten report (Independent Commission for Policing,1999). However, it may also include an enhanced role for the IPCC and the Policing Panel, created in 2011, who are responsible for ensuring the IPCC is held to account for his/her decisions.

Concerns regarding accountability in a world of pluralised policing are real enough. There have been several instances where private security companies involved in public 'policing' activities appear to have been found wanting. One interesting case, for example, concerns private security firm, Close Protection UK, and the way in which it is alleged to have treated contracted stewards. It was reported that the security company had used unpaid jobseekers to steward the Queen's Diamond Jubilee celebrations in London, and that these stewards were asked to sleep under London Bridge before the river pageant the following day. Whatever the truth of the situation surrounding this incident, it was the response from both the company and the government to the allegations that is of interest, particularly in the wider context of using private companies to provide policing activities. In response to the complaints, the company stated it had launched an investigation of its own, while the government regarded the occurrence as a 'one-off' and an 'isolated incident' not worthy of note. Clearly, this matter caused concern for all involved and some politicians were perturbed enough to raise the issue; indeed, it highlights wider concerns regarding public accountability when public policing activities are carried out by private companies. For the government, however, this incident appeared to be insignificant and it was reluctant to become involved. This attitude may not bode well for accountability in any future privatisation or pluralisation of policing activities, especially when individuals or private companies are called to account for their actions.

Conclusion

Defining plural policing can be problematic not least because of the different terminology used to describe the concept. However, pluralised policing is not confined purely to England and Wales and has, to a greater or lesser extent, found its place in many countries. In other countries, this approach is currently less popular, because profit making is seen as being incompatible with the ideals of impartial justice and universal service intrinsic to modern policing.

Despite criticism of the future of pluralised policing, it would appear that private sector policing is likely to be an approach of increasing prominence in a mixed economy of policing provision, both as a low-cost front-line preventative presence and in specialist corporate operations. The next chapter examines the important idea of private policing.

Further reading
Crawford, A. (2014) 'Police, policing and the future of the policing family', in J.M. Brown (ed) *The Future of Policing*, Abingdon: Routledge.

Crawford, A., Lister, S., Blackburn, S. and Burnett, J. (2005) *Plural Policing: The Mixed Economy of Visible Patrols in England and Wales*, Bristol: Policy Press.

Frevel, B. (2015) 'Pluralisation of local policing in Germany: security between the state's monopoly of force and the market', *European Journal of Policing Studies*, vol 2, no 3, pp 267-84.

Independent Commission for Policing. (1999) *A new beginning: Policing in Northern Ireland*, Belfast, Ireland: HMSO.

Jones, T. and Newburn, T. (2002) 'The transformation of policing', *British Journal of Criminology*, vol 42, no 1, pp 128-46.

Jones, T. and Newburn, T. (2006) *Plural Policing: A Comparative Perspective*, Abingdon: Routledge.

Lister, S. and Jones, T. (2015) 'Plural policing and the challenge of democratic accountability', in S. Lister and M. Rowe (eds) *Accountability of Policing*, Abingdon: Routledge.

Loader, I. (2000) 'Plural policing and democratic governance', *Social and Legal Studies*, vol 9, no 3, pp 323-45.

Millie, A. (2012) 'The policing task and the expansion (and contraction) of British policing', *British Journal of Criminology*, vol 52, no 6, pp 1092-1112.

Punch, M., (2011) *Shoot to kill: Police, firearms and fatal force*, Policy Press, Bristol.

Terpstra, J. and Van Stokkom, B. (2015) 'Plural policing in comparative perspective: four models of regulation', *European Journal of Policing Studies*, vol 2, no 3, pp 325-43.

Terpstra, J., Van Stokkom, B. and Spreeuwers, R. (2013) *Who Patrols the Streets?*, The Hague: Eleven International Publishing.

THREE

Private policing

Introduction

The recognition that the concepts of 'police' and 'policing' must be defined and understood separately means that there is now quite a lot of scholarly and practical debate concerning how policing activities take place, which also serves to increase our understanding of how the state and market forces work in this area. However, we need to fully appreciate the problems attached to what many people mean when they refer to the concept of 'private policing'. The first area for consideration is the regulation of private policing and the organisation known as the Security Industry Authority (SIA).

The Security Industry Authority is the organisation responsible for regulating the private security industry in England and Wales. It is an independent body that reports to the Home Secretary, under the terms of the Private Security Industry Act 2001. Its role is to regulate the private security industry effectively, to reduce criminality, raise standards and recognise quality service.

The SIA has two main duties. One is to ensure the compulsory licensing of individuals undertaking designated activities within the private security industry, and the other is to manage the voluntary Approved Contractor Scheme, which measures private security suppliers against independently assessed criteria.

SIA licensing covers manned guarding (including security guarding, door supervision, close protection, cash and valuables in transit, and public space surveillance using CCTV), key holding and vehicle immobilising. Licensing should, it is argued, ensure that private security operatives are 'fit and proper' persons who are properly trained and qualified to do their job.

The Approved Contractor Scheme introduced a set of operational and performance standards for suppliers of private security services. Those organisations that meet these standards are awarded Approved Contractor status. This accreditation provides those who purchase private security services with independent proof of a contractor's commitment to quality.

Despite this regulation and Act of Parliament, it is difficult to gauge the total number of private police and security guards that exist in England and Wales today. Official figures state that some 143,800 people were employed in the investigation and security-related industry in the UK in 2004, and industry experts claim that this has been expanding by three per cent per annum. Other estimates put the figure at 500,000 people employed in the UK private security industry (with up to 350,000 employed in its vertical strand and some 150,000 in the horizontal strand that overlaps with other sectors). No matter which figure you accept, the private security sector is substantial, particularly when compared with the number of police officers in England and Wales, which as we have seen is being reduced.

An example of a private policing security scheme can be seen in Box 3.1.

Box 3.1: Example of private policing

Two former detectives have set up Britain's first private police force to fight crime – costing residents £1 a week. The civilian security officers will patrol a neighbourhood in Stoke, Staffs, and 24-hours a day in a bid to tackle rising yob behaviour as cop numbers are slashed by government. Ex-officers Stewart Brown, 56, and Stephen Rowney, 50, are behind the controversial scheme which they claim will 'fill a gap in the market.'

But the idea has been slammed by police representatives and politicians who fear it will 'undermine' the real boys in blue. Now the company are meeting Staffordshire's Police and Crime Commissioner Matthew Ellis – who is not in favour of people paying for the service – to try to get him to back the proposal. The scheme, the first in the country, will be trialled across North Staffordshire with residents in the Hartshill and Penkhull areas of Stoke-on-Trent already being briefed about the service. Stewart, who retired from the force in 2010 after 33 years with the police, said: "This is another level of policing. Policing should be carried out by officers but unfortunately the demand for services, along with budget reductions, means they can only do so much. The demand on these services is increasing every day."

Now the private firm is seeking to have access to the police force's radio network, dish out on-the-spot fines and also wear police-approved uniforms and drive marked vehicles. In return for the £1-a-week charge, an alarm will be installed which gives residents the chance to alert the firm immediately. At least 700 people are needed to sign up for the scheme.

Stewart, 56, said: "There is a huge gap in the market for this. If you ring 999 to say someone has attempted to break in to your property, the police are unlikely to come immediately unless there is a risk to an individual. It is supply and demand. When I started as a policeman in 1977, the cops went to everything. Now you are lucky if you see one in a day." Ahead of the meeting, Commissioner Ellis said: "If there is anything that involves residents paying for services that I believe the police should be providing then I would not support it." Police Federation Chairman Andy Adams said: "We hold a unique position in society and this undermines that in some way for me." Hartshill and Harpfields Residents' Association Chairman Reg Edwards said: "If someone is driving a car around and it's well identifiable as a security vehicle, or a street security patrol, then that might act as a deterrent."

Source: Hartshill (2015)

Private security firms are also involved with several police forces in England and Wales at a much higher level of activity. A landmark was created in 2012, for example, when Lincolnshire police signed a £200 million contract with G4S to build and staff a police station. This involved custody services, enquiry officers, a control room and a crime management bureau. Interestingly enough, some 12 companies responded with submissions for the contract, which indicates the readiness of private industry to respond to public sector requirements. The following indicates the reported success of the scheme.

Box 3.2: Lincolnshire and G4S partnership

Police forces in England and Wales could save £1bn a year by outsourcing backroom services to private companies, private security firm G4S has said.

The firm signed a £200m contract with Lincolnshire Police in 2012, with G4S staff now employed in backroom roles.

John Shaw, from G4S, said it has saved the force £6m a year – and other forces could "easily" make similar savings.

The Police Federation of England and Wales said any changes should "not compromise public safety".

Its chairman Steve White also said any savings would have to be reinvested into policing.

Its staff are employed in police control rooms, custody suites, in areas of firearms licensing, as well as in financial, HR and technology roles.

Mr Shaw, the firm's managing director for public services, said the model in Lincolnshire could be replicated elsewhere, potentially saving £1bn a year across all 43 forces.

Source: www.bbc.co.uk/news/uk-34864781 (accessed 17 March 2016)

Prior to the Private Security Industry Act 2001, some specific sectors, such as private prisoner custody, were subject to regulation. However, the private security industry sector was largely subject to no or little specific regulation. The perceived powers of security operatives, the opportunities for abuse, and evidence of criminality among a minority had led to calls for statutory regulation. Therefore, for Crawford (2014), the Act was introduced, in part at least, to place the private security industry into the mainstream of policing services by encouraging a higher degree of professionalism and to regulate unscrupulous operators. In addition, this form of legislation appears to improve the perceived legitimacy of the industry and open up wider markets within the plural policing world.

In November 2012, the government published a paper outlining its preferred options for the future of the regulation of the private security industry (Home Office, 2012). This document outlined how there would be a change in how individuals were to be licensed and a phased transition to a business regulation approach within the industry.

Currently (2106), there is an ongoing consolation programme surrounding the future of the SIA, with the government considering a review of the organisation.

The review will examine:

- how the SIA contributes to the core business of the Home Office and to the delivery of wider cross-government priorities;
- SIA's capacity and capability to deliver more effectively and efficiently, including identifying the potential for efficiency savings;
- incentives for controlling costs and driving efficiencies – are they sufficient? Is there further scope to achieve these?;
- the SIA's performance in ensuring any burdens on the regulated sector are demonstrably proportionate and necessary;
- how customers' priorities for the SIA services are built into SIA strategic planning processes; and

- the scope and appropriateness of the SIA taking on additional functions including those that may already be provided by other organisations or functions that could further enhance the SIA's role (www.gov.uk/government/consultations/review-of-the-security-industry-authority-sia, accessed 17 March 2016).

Clearly, it appears that the current government wishes to position the security industry nearer to the centre of delivery of private security provision as part of the plural policing approach.

'Private-ness' and policing services

There have been many attempts to categorise just exactly what constitutes private policing. Prenzler and Wakefield (2009) point to the fact that private policing is a confused concept that carries many different meanings. It variants include such terms as 'outsourcing', 'commercialisation', 'user-payers' and 'deregulation', but at its simplest it refers to a process in which government-owned assets or services are wholly or partially transferred to private companies. Button (2002) also points out the difference in terminology used and highlights the increasing use of the word 'commercial' rather than privatisation regarding non-public policing. However, some public policing involves commercial work (income generation) so the use of the word 'private' generally presents fewer problems of definition. On the face of it, the difference between public and private seems quite obvious, they being distinguished by the sector to which they belong. If the police are part of the services provided by government and funded by taxpayers they are public, but if their services are provided as a result of fees paid to companies they are private. In between these sits a grey area, sometimes referred to as 'quasi-policing'.

The rise of the 'quasi-police'

The term 'quasi-policing' has been used to convey the fact that many police and prison service functions have been devolved from state bodies to specially empowered civilians. These individuals perform certain functions more commonly associated with police and prison officers. They focus on specific security duties as opposed to general security duties undertaken by private security companies, such as patrolling office blocks, shopping malls and other commercial outlets. While most of the 'quasi-police' are part of the private security industry, they operate at specific sites and undertake specific activities. The duties they undertake are varied and one example in particular, the issue of Channel Tunnel security, is briefly discussed below.

Channel Tunnel security

The Treaty of Canterbury, signed by the UK and France 1986, established the need for the defence of the Channel Fixed Link, and this was incorporated into domestic legislation through the Channel Tunnel (Security) Order 1994. The order requires the tunnel operators and any trains that transit the tunnel to apply counter-terrorist security measures.

Operators are also responsible for the day-to-day delivery of security, which includes screening vehicles, passengers, baggage and freight, among other measures. The department's compliance officers ensure that the security arrangements in place meet the statutory requirements and standards by regular monitoring and testing. Security measures are closely tailored to the potential risks of each situation, taking account of the threat as assessed by the government's security advisers and the vulnerability of the system.

The following is a key excerpt from the Channel Tunnel (Security) Order 1994.

> The Secretary of State may give a direction in writing to any person to whom this paragraph applies requiring him to take such measures for purposes to which this part of this Order applies as are specified in the direction.
>
> (a) in the case of a direction given to a person as the owner, operator or train manager of a Channel Tunnel train, in respect of all the trains falling within paragraph (1) (a) above of which (at the time when the direction is given or at any subsequent time) he is the owner, operator or train manager, or in respect of any such trains specified in the direction,
> (b) in the case of a direction given to the Concessionaires, in respect of the tunnel system,
> (c) in the case of a direction given to a person as a person falling within paragraph (1) (c) above, in respect of the operations carried on by him,
> (d) in the case of a direction given to a person as a person who is permitted to have access to a restricted zone as mentioned in paragraph (1) (d) above, in respect of such

activities carried on by that person in that zone as are specified in the direction, and

(e) in the case of a direction given to a person as the owner, operator or manager of any property used in connection with the operation of any Channel Tunnel train or the tunnel system, in respect of all the property falling within paragraph (1) (e) above of which at the time when the direction is given he is the owner, operator or manager, or in respect of any such property as is specified in the direction.

The empowerment of certain civilians as well as police to conduct searches in fulfilment of these requirements is clearly indicated by the words 'persons of a description specified in the direction' and 'persons so specified'.

In addition to the examples provided, there has in the past two decades been a substantial rise in quasi-policing carried out by people in other roles, including magistrates, court security officers, prisoner custody officers, and those working in immigration removal centres.

However, despite the proliferation of quasi-police, the issue of accountability – for officers' actions and use of force, as well as for third-party interventions in general – remains problematic. Issues surrounding just who is responsible and which structures apply are important considerations, and the essential topic of accountability is discussed more widely in the following chapter. Understanding the complexities of private policing has led many commentators to attempt to classify exactly what it entails. When discussing the ideas of private-ness, Benn and Gaus (1983) highlight three dimensions: access, agency and whose interest is served. We examine these briefly in turn.

Access

This dimension is sub-divided into four further categories, as seen in Table 3.1.

Agency

This aspect concerns the status of an individual, and is best illustrated in Figure 3.1.

Table 3.1: Access and private policing

Physical access	Public – beaches, parks, public spaces. Private – private locations, controlled access, gated communities.
Access to activities	Public – meetings open to the public. Private – restricted to members only.
Access to information	Public – open to anyone on public websites. Private – intranet-style facilities for staff only.
Access to resources	Public – water, food and so on for whole community. Private – resources for certain residents only.

Figure 3.1: Individuals' status and private policing

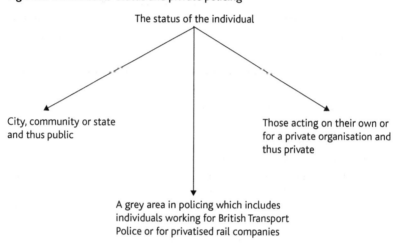

The status of the individual

City, community or state and thus public

Those acting on their own or for a private organisation and thus private

A grey area in policing which includes individuals working for British Transport Police or for privatised rail companies

Interests served

In simple terms, this relates to the body that is served by the particular activity. A private interest supports a specific individual, group or organisation, while a public interest involves an individual or organisation that seeks to benefit all.

As we can see, the distinction between public and private is a complicated one, especially when we start to enter the realms of policing provision.

Johnston (1992) referred to the patchwork of policing provision as that of 'hybrid policing'. Hybrid policing contains a range of organisations whose formal status and operating territories cut across the public–private divide. Some are organised uniformed forces, while others are merely agents with the right to exert specific legal powers in given situations.

Johnson provides a classification of his idea of hybrid policing, which is summarised in Table 3.2.

Table 3.2: Classification of hybrid policing bodies

Bodies engaged in functions related to state security	Including immigration staff, prison officers, Ministry of Defence police, and various military police forces.
Special police forces	Including police forces created under legislation other than by the Police Act 1964, such as British Transport Police and various parks and docks police forces.
Departments of state	Including some of the many officials engaged in regulatory, investigative and law enforcement functions employed by government departments, such as HM Revenue and Customs and other investigative units.
Municipal bodies	Including local authority staff engaged in regulatory and investigative functions such as environmental health officers, social workers and so on.
Miscellaneous regulating and investigative bodies	This includes all other bodies such as Post Office investigators and BBC investigators.

There are clear problems with the use of the term 'hybrid policing' as it can be utilised to describe both public and private bodies that are neither the public police, private security nor some form of voluntary initiative. As Button (2002) suggests, there is a need to break down the wide range of organisations that fall into the 'hybrid' category. Further, the term 'hybrid policing' has been criticised by Jones and Newburn (2006), who believe the phrase was created in response to the problems of resolving the public–private dichotomy. Their attempt to classify policing provision tends to ignore a significant number of private organisations engaged in policing activities that are not private security. Nonetheless, they suggest four distinct classifications as follows:

• Home Office police forces, such as the Metropolitan Police Service;
• other bodies of constabulary, for example, British Transport Police, parks police;
• other public police, for example, in the areas of environmental health and benefits fraud;
• private security, for example, staffed services providing guards and door supervisors, investigative services and installers of security equipment.

Pirie (1988) points to the fact that the concept of privatisation was little used before 1979, and is a product of the managerialism movement that has swept through industrial countries since the 1980s in the drive for greater efficiency in public sector management. The justification behind this approach has been that commercial competition and the profit motive provide powerful incentives for more efficient and better-quality services to the public. Outsourcing or 'contracting out' is considered to be the situation whereby the police enter into contracts with third parties to purchase goods or services with them. It is a long-standing approach and has involved the purchase of police equipment, cleaning services, catering and so on. However, other areas of police work, including custodial and prisoner escort, are also now subject to outsourcing. This situation opens up whole new areas of business for the private security industry.

Private security can be seen to encompass all crime prevention, law enforcement and investigative activities carried out on a contractual commercial basis or within private firms. In other words, it concerns those policing and protective services not provided by public sector police that are funded by taxation and delivered free of charge to the public. It also excludes security activities provided on a voluntary or non-commercial basis. Therefore, citizens in their security interactions, such as at sports grounds, shopping centres and airports, are far more likely to encounter private security personnel than police officers.

Private sector involvement in partnerships

Police and Crime Commissioner (PCC) and chief constable posts are now situated in separate corporate bodies. PCCs receive grants from central government, determined by the specific needs of their areas. PCCs also raise revenue to fund their police forces' operations by levying a precept on council tax collection authorities, which is added to local people's council tax bills. The ratio of central government to local taxpayer funding varies between forces; as such, changes to central government funding following the 2010 comprehensive spending review affected forces differently. In total, the specified reduction in central government funding is £2.1 billion in real terms (£1.2 billion in cash terms) in 2014/15, compared with funding in 2010/11. What this all means is that the police and the PCC have the power to engage in partnerships with the private sector for the provision of policing services.

The private sector is an important aspect of society, creating job opportunities as well as helping to enhance the social and economic skills and development of people within communities. It can also stimulate innovative projects, particularly involving crime reduction. Businesses, factories and other commercial premises can be significantly affected by high levels of crime and violence within neighbourhoods and cities, thus helping to reduce such activity is in their own interests. It is interesting to examine just why the private sector is so well placed to contribute to community wellbeing and general safety improvement.

First, private firms, which are relatively new to the concept of community safety partnerships, can be an excellent breeding ground for new ideas that stimulate other partner members. A private company may be best placed to coordinate other businesses, public and private members of the community and other stakeholders to work on joint prevention projects. This approach could also contribute to ensuring the sustainability of projects, including introducing economies of scale (which makes things more affordable), and ownership of projects by local communities.

Second, private companies can establish themselves as models of good practice for other businesses, and for the community as a whole. This status is important in the world of business, but in turn businesses must ensure that they are compliant with many laws, such as those governing racial discrimination and negative advertising among others.

Third, private sector firms often have easier access to key information, the media and public authorities and are therefore in a unique position to be heard. It is important for them to keep track of projects and policies aimed at reducing crime and disorder in their areas, and to use this advantageous position to promote and support good ideas that aim to achieve the same outcomes.

Fourth, private companies generally have resources that other sectors lack. Businesses tend to have greater flexibility than the public sector to provide jobs, and are usually prepared to recruit workers from vulnerable groups such as young people.

Finally, private business may have funds that are more readily available and can be used to support projects undertaken by community safety partners. They may also be able to contribute financially towards improving crime and disorder reduction projects and assisting with training and effective action plans.

In addition, private companies can also offer a more objective, independent approach to community safety projects, with the ability to provide innovation in terms of solutions to problems. Public–private partnerships (PPPs) are increasingly used for co-financing in the development, construction and maintenance of public works and initiatives. However, this approach is not a new one. The United

Nations guidelines on crime prevention (United Nations, 1991) specifically mention the role of the private sector in community safety, as partners with national and local governments (as providers of services such as housing construction). Again, these documents emphasise the social contribution private companies are able to make to communities, highlighting how they can achieve this by engaging in a wide range of projects. These include violence reduction, situational and design opportunities to reduce criminality, urban renewal projects, the development of learning programmes and the provision of job training and employment opportunities to prevent recidivism.

The idea of PPPs is an appealing one in the current political and economic climate, and appears to be a way of extending the current community safety partnership approach to crime prevention and reduction.

The police have contracted with the private sector for several decades, but this activity has increased recently and some forces have now agreed high-value, long-term contracts. In its report *Policing in Austerity: One Year On* (HMIC, 2012b), Her Majesty's Inspectorate of Constabulary identified that these arrangements can help forces develop new and more efficient approaches to providing services. However, such partnerships can also heighten operational and financial risks.

Key learning points identified in the HMIC report so far are as follows:

- **Strategy, objectives and service outcomes.** Forces had clear strategies, objectives and outcomes and had communicated these clearly to the market. They identified their risk appetites and tolerance levels. Forces had strong leaders who recognised where there were shortages of commercial skills and expertise. Forces and PCCs should consider how they will develop detailed service specifications. They should understand what cost and performance analyses will help to align these to organisational priorities, drawing on benchmarking data where available. They will also benefit from developing their relationship with their potential partners and understanding each other's culture and values.
- **Sourcing and tender evaluation stages.** Forces undertook their sourcing stage and tender evaluation effectively and recorded their scoring decisions. Forces and PCCs should consider issues of contract flexibility early on. They should also baseline their costs and performance as far as possible. However, we recognise that they did this during the sourcing phase and improved

their business understanding. Those forces and PCCs entering into partnerships should be aware that these activities are resource-intensive and should weigh the advantages gained against the costs incurred.

- **Governance, leadership and stakeholder management.** Forces described senior leadership as a catalyst for ensuring that projects had impetus and direction. Forces were aware of when they needed external support and recognised that partners could bring innovative approaches to stakeholder management. Forces and PCCs entering a partnership should consider what, and how, they will communicate with their stakeholders and make sure that they respond to their feedback. This will help stakeholders to support the project as far as possible and achieve optimal outcomes.
- **Contract and performance management.** Forces stated that they had effective contract and performance management and made sure that they had robust recording practices. Forces cited several benefits of good contract management, which included informal dialogue and feedback, greater professionalism and resolving issues effectively. We suggest that forces and PCCs assess how they intend to monitor performance. They should then decide whether to pursue service credits, wherever the contract provides, or a more flexible approach during periods of complex change. These decisions should be agreed and documented. Forces and PCCs should also understand how they will get feedback from end-users to review these decisions and should review their approach to performance appraisal regularly. (HMIC, 2012b, p 61)

However, PPPs are not without their problems. As Corvellec (2009) highlights, there are substantial risks associated with the PPP approach. PPPs tend to be contractual relationships between public authorities and the world of business that aim to ensure the funding, construction, renovation, management or maintenance of an infrastructure or the provision of a service (Commission of the European Communities, 2004). Consequently, public bodies purchase a raft of services under specified terms and conditions. In addition, there is a risk that is shared equally between the public and private partnership, based on a shared commitment to achieve a desired public policy outcome. In particular, this relates to risks from a rise in operating costs and the rise in inflation or exchange rates. The political rationale of PPPs, clearly, is to achieve the best possible value for public money, coupled with the promise, as we have seen, of better accountability, better on-time and on-budget delivery and a more innovative public sector. However, an analysis by Hodge and Greve (2009) casts some doubt on the veracity of such claims regarding PPPs. Examining many PPPs, these authors suggest that little or poor evaluation of PPPs' achievement of their stated aims means that there is some question over their 'value for money' claims.

In terms of accountability, there are also great differences between PPPs and public bodies. Hebson and colleagues (2003), in their study of PPPs in the health service, point to the fact that private sector managers stressed that they were accountable to their shareholders but tended to disguise this view in the practical world of partnerships, as a high level of trust between partners accountable to each other was deemed to be more important. However, this image of high-trust relationships was challenged by public sector managers. It would appear that as time passed, public service managers no longer had confidence in the ability of private sector managers to self-monitor their standards of service delivery.

The police had always worked with the private sector before the 2008 global financial crisis and subsequent years of austerity. However, currently this work is more extensive, with the most recent examples involving Cleveland Police and Lincolnshire Police. In these forces, business support services as well as control room and criminal justice services are provided by the private sector in partnership with the force. Despite this, the HMIC (2013) report on policing in austerity expressed deep disappointment that more collaboration and PPPs had not occurred. It highlighted that the pace of change had been too slow and only a minority of forces up to that point were redelivering more than 10 per cent of their savings through collaboration. Despite this, current police–private partnerships are keen to highlight their success. For example, the partnership between Lincolnshire Police and G4S has suggested that extensive savings are possible as can be seen in Box 3.3.

Box 3.3: Media release for G4S and Lincolnshire Police

- New report shows Lincolnshire Police Service partnership with private sector is improving service and delivering greater savings than forecast
- One year into the ten-year partnership with G4S, estimated savings are over 18% or £5m per annum, equivalent to cost of 125 police officers

- If every force spent the same per head of population as Lincolnshire, the national police grant could be reduced by £1 billion
- Crime across Lincolnshire has been reduced by 14%

A unique partnership between the police and the private sector could be the key to unlocking valuable funds for cash-strapped police forces, according to a new report published today by G4S, Lincolnshire Police and the Police and Crime Commissioner (PCC), Alan Hardwick. One year on from the start of the G4S-Lincolnshire Police Strategic Partnership, which saw the bulk of the force's organisational services transferred to G4S, Lincolnshire Police has been able to make estimated savings of 18 per cent – more than the 13.6 per cent originally guaranteed by G4S.

The savings achieved mean Lincolnshire now spends the lowest amount per head of population on policing in England and Wales. According to Lincolnshire's PCC, Alan Hardwick, if the other 42 forces in England and Wales could achieve this level of spending, the savings to the national purse would amount to £1 billion.

Source: BBC (2015b).

It has been claimed that this success was achieved with no detrimental effect to the service provided; indeed, in many areas, real service improvements, such as in the response to 999 calls, have been measured by the police force. Further, it was expected that the many forces around the country facing difficult decisions about how to maintain services in the face of constricting budgets would approach both Lincolnshire Police and G4S to benefit from their experiences.

On the other hand, there have also been occasions where the PPP approach involving the police has not been successful. Following the 2012 Olympic Games in London, where a substantial amount of private–public security and policing took place, multimillion pound plans by three police forces to outsource services to the firm at the centre of the Olympics security collapsed. Hertfordshire Police and Crime Commissioner David Lloyd stated that the Bedfordshire, Cambridgeshire and Hertfordshire Strategic Alliance had discontinued negotiations with G4S. Prior to this, the three forces had been considering working with G4S in a bid to save £73 million by outsourcing support functions, with the proposals involving the transfer of 1,100 roles, including human resources, IT and finance to the security contractor.

It would appear that doubts were raised after the company was forced to admit severe failings over the Olympics security contract, which led to police officers and 3,500 extra military troops being deployed to support the operation. The Police and Crime Commissioner for Bedfordshire, Olly Martins, agreed with the decision as he felt the contract did not deliver what was needed.

There are, of course, many reasons why private–public partnerships may not live up to expectations. However, White (2015) suggests that there are five main reasons why it is difficult for the police to engage in successful partnerships with the private sector.

1. Media scaremongering

No police force in the UK, at any point, has sold off its front-line services to the private sector. Forces have been contracting out *some* of these services – such as custody, call handling and managing police station front counters – to the private sector for a limited duration. So 'privatisation' is probably the wrong word to describe this 'contracting out' taking place within some police forces, since it implies a far greater degree of market penetration than has actually occurred. 'Outsourcing' is a much better word. However, the media have placed the debate within a 'privatisation' framework and have implied that private companies are gradually taking over the public police service, which tends to invoke fear and uncertainty in the public.

2. Public fear

The reason behind the effectiveness of such media scaremongering is the fear, among many members of the public, of what might happen if police forces are over-exposed to the market. We have often witnessed public outrage directed towards instances of police malpractice or incompetence, but at another level it seems that most citizens actually respect and support the police. Uniformed police officers give talks in schools to educate young people about the protective role of the police in a civilised society. They also raise awareness of other types of social crime prevention activities, which affects what is a complex yet generally positive relationship between the citizen and the police. Privatising – or outsourcing – the police also tends to promote fear and anxiety among the public who are used to receiving their policing services from the public police.

3. Resistance from within

The oft-discussed and enduring principle of constabulary independence means that, if they so wish, the 43 police forces in England and Wales can do things in 43 different ways, and in general this has been applied to the concept of outsourcing services to the public. Some forces have embraced outsourcing; others have rejected it outright because there are structural factors at play. Some are better placed than others to deal with austerity measures imposed from within their force, meaning more savings can be made through internal rationalisation. However, there is another key factor at work. Cultural resistance to change from within the police may, in part, be responsible for a general lack of engagement with the market, and the reason why some forces have sought other solutions to their financial predicament. This means that in some forces outsourcing never enters the agenda as a matter of principle. Those forces that do entertain this option may be faced with resistance not only from the public, but from their colleagues too.

4. Inexperience in the contracting-out process

The world of public sector outsourcing is a complex one, especially for an institution such as the police, which has minimal experience of its intricacies. When putting together a proposal, interested private sector providers will want to know the business processes and unit costs of every single service included in the invitation for tender. However, police forces generally tend not to think in these terms, being focused, naturally enough perhaps, on victims and criminals, evidence and arrests. Gathering the necessary information for the contracting-out process can therefore be a long and painstaking task of self-examination that may never reach a conclusion. In the past, some police forces have had to come to this realistion; Surrey Police and West Midlands Police, for example, both discovered that these complexities played a part when their controversial £1.5 billion outsourcing deal did not come to fruition after years of effort.

5. Staffing the contract

There is a further problem for those forces that have been successful in the process of outsourcing, such as Lincolnshire Police. Despite the major transformation in Lincolnshire Police's organisational structure, some things do not appear to have changed significantly. This is in part a matter of choice. Lincolnshire Police have been careful to strike a balance between protecting their distinctive public service ethos and obtaining benefits from the business-process knowledge and outsourcing expertise of G4S. However, it is also to some extent a consequence of how the contract has been staffed. G4S have not replaced Lincolnshire Police staff with G4S staff but have instead inherited the Lincolnshire Police staff already in position. This means that, in many instances, the individual responsible for delivering the outsourced service has worked for Lincolnshire Police for their entire working life, and approaches the job with exactly the same attitude they held before G4S became involved in the policing provision in Lincolnshire. Apart from a change in uniform perhaps, staff see no real difference and therefore their attitude and cultural values may remain the same.

For partnerships, in whatever format they take, close cooperation is essential to ensure that the public receive the correct level of service, which includes ensuring that more crime is reported rather than remaining hidden and unreported. Further, with information being shared between public and private agencies, repeat offences can be easily identified and action taken immediately to prevent re-victimisation. Such strategies, it is hoped, will make sure that victims' rights are placed firmly on the local, national and political agenda. However, this type of approach has failed to transform some practices, and victims' feelings about the criminal justice system remain on the whole negative. While many current partnerships have a relationship with victims that involves purely notifying and supplying information to them, it is suggested that victims could play a greater part in the policy formation that guides the involvement of many partnerships in crime prevention.

The current government's approach

The current focus of the ongoing debate on the pluralisation of policing appears to be the economic austerity of recent years. Clearly, however, the pluralisation of policing services began well before this. Clearly, however, the pluralisation of policing services is far older than that. The current Conservative government, against a backdrop of fiscal austerity, has implemented the largest cuts to public services since the 1980s. Most notably, this approach included an examination of the structure of the police and local authorities. Their capacity and scope for partnership involvement and delivery could be expected to be different from previous ways of working. Reforms were being implemented across all of the organisations apart from the London Fire and Rescue Services. At the same time, the Coalition government was developing the concept of the 'Big Society', which focused on decentralisation and the redistribution of power to communities. In essence, this approach involves handing down power to local authorities and the communities they serve. It also seeks to engage with the voluntary sector much more than previously.

Comments made by MP Nick Herbert, the minister for policing, are largely supportive of partnership working, although he promised further improvements. At the National Community Safety Network Conference in March 2011, he confirmed that CSPs would continue, and would provide the partnership framework for addressing crime and disorder at the local level (Herbert, 2011). Despite this show of support, however, there was also confirmation that partnerships had to be more effective with 'more action and less meetings'. They had to be clear about the fact that there would be no 'magic chequebook' (Herbert, 2011).

To provide more flexibility and freedom, the Coalition government reduced the number of regulations placed on each CSP. This was a response to the publication of the consultation document *Policing in the 21st Century: Reconnecting Police and the People* in July 2010 (Home Office, 2010) in which the government outlined its proposals for police reform. A key section, entitled 'Tackling Crime Together', outlines the government's commitment to improving the partnership between the police and the public and helping partners work together to solve local issues. This is further evidence of the government's approach to reducing prescription and bureaucracy. One of the coalition's key structural reform priorities included the introduction of directly elected PCCs (Home Office, 2011). The key messages from central government revolved around the idea that CSPs should have no national targets, and needed to rely more on their local communities rather than Whitehall for advice on prioritising crime issues. It appears that there will be no external quality assurance, with the PCCs instead having a monitoring role and being used to greater involve the public, and a scrutiny role being given to local councillors (Local Government Association, 2012).

With local authority boundaries under consideration of review in parts of the country, and the political will to rationalise public services for reasons of economic efficiency and effectiveness, the geographic considerations for community safety partnership work may need to be revisited. This will again produce an opportunity to revise the make-up of the partnership approach to crime prevention, and once more we may see a growth in the number of PPPs engaged in that form of activity.

In terms of PPPs between the police and the private sector, as austerity bites further, and the political will remains to reduce the amount of resources for the public police, the growth of public–private involvement in a growing range of police activities seems inevitable.

Conclusion

This chapter, along with the preceding chapters, has sought to highlight how the public police will not be alone in carrying out policing activity in the future. Given recent trends, the future of policing will probably become more pluralised and multifaceted. This is more the case in England and Wales than in continental Europe where the private security industry has gained less momentum. Clearly, private policing institutions are varied in their scope and activities and are already situated within the world of policing, but plural policing and its extension will depend in part on the role and view of the PCCs. However, the increasing prominence of the SIA and its development into a business-controlling authority may suggest an expanding role for the private sector in the future.

Further reading
Button. M. (2002) *Private policing*, Cullompton: Willan.

Commission of the European Communities, (2004), Brussels, available at http://ec.europa.eu/information_society/doc/qualif/health/COM_2004_0356_F_EN_ACTE.pdf

HMIC (2012) *Policing in austerity: One year on*, London, HMIC.

Home Office (2010) *Policing in the 21st century: Reconnecting police and the people*, available at https://www.gov.uk/government/uploads/system/uploads/attachment_data/file/118241/policing-21st-full-pdf.pdf

Johnston, L. (1992) *The Rebirth of Private Policing*, London: Routledge.

Jones, T. and Newburn, T. (2002) *Private Security and Private Policing*, Oxford: Oxford University Press.

Local Government Association, (2012) *Police and Crime Commissioners: A guide for councils*, available at http://www.local.gov.uk/c/document_library/get_file?uuid=7aae958c-9da7-44ee-8ebc-9fe2d772fc0c&groupId=10180

Shearing, C.D. and Stenning, P.C. (1981) 'Modern private security: its growth and implications', in M. Tonry and N. Morris (eds) *Crime and Justice: An Annual Review of Research, Vol 3*, Chicago, IL: University of Chicago Press.

Shearing, C.D. and Stenning, P.C. (1983) 'Private security: implications for social control', *Social Problems*, vol 30, no 5, pp 498-505.

UNODC (United Nations Office on Drugs and Crime) (2011) 'Civilian private security services: their role, oversight and contribution to crime prevention and community safety', available at www.unodc.org/documents/justice-and-prison-reform/Expert-group-meeting-Bangkok/IEGMCivilianPrivateSecurity/UNODC_CCPCJ_EG.5_2011_1_English.pdf (accessed 26 November 2015).

Van Steden, R. (2007) *Privatising policing: Describing and explaining the growth of private security*, The Hague: Boom Juridische Uitgevers.

Part 2
Public plural policing in England and Wales

This section concentrates on the way plural policing has developed on a practical level in England and Wales over the past decade or so. In particular, it focuses on the way public policing has evolved into a plural form of policing. It examines the ideas behind the introduction of neighbourhood policing teams, which have been the prime example of a form of plural policing for some time, and considers the constituent parts of this approach. In particular, the section explores the introduction of police community support officers, the continued use of volunteers, including the special constabulary, and the idea of community safety partnership work as being within the concept of public 'plural policing'.

FOUR

Neighbourhood policing teams

Introduction

It is tempting to think of plural policing as a relatively recent concept, brought about by austerity measures and recent political philosophy changes in government. Moreover, the pluralised approach tends to be associated with a reliance on the private sector. However, the delivery of policing services by unsworn officers – those who are not constables, in other words – has been a feature of the policing landscape for some time, particularly at the local level. Indeed, one approach, known as neighbourhood policing, has apparently been so successful that it is considered to be the bedrock of community policing in England and Wales, albeit now in decline as a result of austerity measures. This public-oriented approach to pluralised policing is therefore worthy of attention as it may provide us with lessons for the future of plural policing involving private policing organisations.

Historical context

The UK has a long tradition of 'consensus' policing as encapsulated in the famous principle 'the police are the public and the public are the police' (see Peak and Glensor, 1996, for example). During the second half of the 20th century, the gap between the police and the communities they served began to widen, as car patrols replaced foot patrols and police stations began to work on reduced opening hours or were permanently closed. In the UK, it has been suggested that the introduction of unit beat policing contributed to this negative perception (Rogers, 2004). As a response to this widening gap, community policing began to emerge in a number of forces across the UK. Meanwhile, similar developments were occurring in the 1970s and early 1980s in other countries, especially North America and the Netherlands. John Alderson, a former chief constable, argued strongly at the time that policing should evolve from being a traditional and 'authoritarian' profession to one that aspires to the greater involvement of the community. The principles underpinning community policing have been widely adopted and community policing has become, in the US at least, 'a new orthodoxy for cops' (Eck and Rosenbaum, 1994). Albeit a difficult concept to describe, the following provides a reasonable definition:

> Community policing is the delivery of police services through a customer-focused approach, utilising partnerships to maximise community resources in a problem-solving format to prevent crime, reduce the fear of crime, apprehend those involved in criminal activity, and improve a community's quality of life. (Morash and Ford, 2002, p 4)

The most comprehensive example of a carefully evaluated community policing programme in the US is the Chicago Alternative Policing Strategy (CAPS), which has had a considerable influence on the development of neighbourhood policing in the UK.

Policing 'Chicago-style'

Much of the academic literature based on the 'Chicago-style' of policing can be found in the works of Wesley Skogan (Skogan, 1990; 1992; 1998; 2006a; 2006b). The origin of this approach can be traced back to 1993 when CAPS became a subject of interest and research. Initially, the CAPS idea was introduced in five police districts, all with diverse communities. The concept involved the police seeking a reduction in local concerns about crime, through working with other agencies in the area to address the issues identified by those who lived there. The main ideas behind CAPS can be seen in Table 4.1.

Table 4.1: The components of CAPS

Crime control and crime prevention to become integrated, coupled with rapid response and problem-solving approaches.	Police officers at all levels to receive training in problem-solving, communication and leadership skills.
Specific teams of police officers to engage in proactive problem solving.	Data from neighbourhoods utilised to highlight crime hotspots including the sharing of such data with communities.
Continuity to be introduced through police officers working the same beat continually.	Continuous communication with communities through a variety of methods.
Greater involvement and engagement with the community to identify local issues for attention.	Changing management techniques utilised to implement the crime reduction strategies.
Formulation of beat profiles that include serious problems and identification of agency resources to deal with them.	Independent evaluation of the process and the outcomes of the CAPS programme.

While the CAPS programme was obviously influential, in the UK the foundation of neighbourhood policing was also influenced by other factors. In particular, the Scarman report (Scarman, 1981), published following the Brixton disorders in 1980, exposed problems in community relations between the police and the community. Specifically, the report identified that the police service had become unresponsive to community needs and uncommunicative to the community more generally. Policing was police-centric rather than community-centric, and there was an obvious need for the police to move towards a service ethos (Savage, 2007). Ultimately, the idea of community policing gained momentum in England and Wales. Initially, this was evident in the 'reassurance policing' approach, and later through neighbourhood policing ideas, both of which have their roots in the wider concept of improving community policing approaches (Fielding, 2009). Reassurance policing became a popular phenomenon in the early 2000s as it became apparent that there was a large gap between the falling crime rate and the public's perception that crime was still rising dramatically. Jansson (2006)highlighted this in the 2005/06 British Crime Survey, which showed that despite falling crime levels, around two thirds of the survey respondents thought that crime had increased in the previous two years. With fear of crime also high, the idea of reassurance policing was developed, initially in Surrey, drawing on the work of Innes (2004; 2007) on signal crimes. The theory behind reassurance policing was that certain types of crime and disorder had a disproportionate impact on fear of crime and perceptions of personal safety, and therefore needed to be addressed by the police as soon as possible.

Prior to this work, however, the Home Office introduced the National Reassurance Policing Programme in 2003. The main aim of this programme was focused less on dealing with crime outcomes than on improving the perceptions of the public. This drew criticism from some quarters, especially when considering that police resources would be dedicated to an activity based on people's perceptions (FitzGerald et al, 2002).

The main aim of the two-year pilot study was to reduce crime and disorder, increase public confidence and satisfaction and narrow the reassurance gap. The programme sought to reduce crime and disorder and improve public confidence through three main methods. These were:

• engaging with communities to identify local concerns and priorities;

- allocating police resources to measures aimed at dealing with these concerns;
- creating a visible and accessible police presence.

Briefly, evaluation suggested that the programme had achieved its aims through a combination of increased numbers of foot patrol officers, community engagement activities and problem-solving initiatives. Because of this success, key components of the programme formed part of the neighbourhood policing approach, particularly the elements of police visibility, problem solving and, of course, engagement with the community.

The political context for the introduction of reassurance through neighbourhood policing is an interesting one. According to Bullock and Sindall (2014), the rationale behind neighbourhood policing lies in the development of a form of governance known as 'new localism'. This approach became prominent towards the end of the 20th century in response to the perceived centralisation of government control, which saw the introduction and use of such measures as key performance indicators and inspections. New localism rejected this imposition from above, believing that policy should be influenced by local needs and its impact on people's daily lives (Stoker, 2006). As a result, neighbourhood policing teams became a focus for implementing such an approach, chiefly by instigating greater levels of communication with the public in an attempt to move citizens closer to the police. In addition, as Crawford and Lister (2004) point out, there was a need to provide signs of visible authority within communities. The task of 'filling the gaps' between demands for visible presence and what could be supplied in order to provide reassurance also forced the government to examine different forms of visible patrol. In addition, there had been and continues to be a decline in the number of occupations with a secondary social control function, as well as a reduction in the number of local institutions of civic engagement. For example, the decline in the number of churches in response to dwindling congregations, a general lack of political participation among citizens and a decline in the governance of public spaces and surveillance by workers such as park keepers, train guards and bus conductors has been considerable (Jones and Newburn, 2002a). These changes have greatly contributed to the general desire for a visible police presence among communities.

The arrival of neighbourhood policing teams

In 2005, the initial Neighbourhood Policing Programme was introduced across all forces in England and Wales, with the introduction of neighbourhood policing teams (NPTs) in every ward. The teams were to consist of a dedicated sergeant with a number of police constables and police community support officers (PCSOs) at his disposal. They were instructed to use a wide range of ideas and techniques to increase community engagement, with the Association of Chief Police Officers (ACPO) producing a practice advice document that would help achieve the success required from the programme (ACPO, 2006). Initially, NPTs were introduced in 43 BCUs (Basic Command Units) across the country as a 'pathfinder' or pilot scheme, with the approach being widely implemented across all forces during the second year, and fully introduced during the third year. A thematic review by Her Majesty's Inspectorate of Constabulary (HMIC) in 2008 found that all forces had achieved the basic aim of making neighbourhood policing a core part of their work (HMIC, 2008).

The HMIC report, while supportive of the approach, also pointed out that there were some issues with the implementation of NPTs. These included the following:

- Boundaries of neighbourhoods were seldom agreed with partners and other agencies, resulting in poor communication and engagement, which in turn did not necessarily meet the needs of the communities.
- Engagement with communities was inconsistent, especially with so-called 'hard-to-reach groups'.
- Community intelligence was not well defined or utilised.
- Joint problem solving between agencies was problematic.

Consequently, the HMIC report produced five major recommendations as follows:

- The duties of the PCSO were to be clarified to increase public awareness of the role.
- Engagement should be flexible and adapt to local circumstances.
- There should be clear guidelines produced by ACPO and the National Police and Improvement Agency regarding the functions of the PCSO.
- Forces should ensure best practice and consistency of approach.
- Forces should review the contact mechanisms for NPTs.

Citizen-focused policing

Given that neighbourhood policing teams are seen as the manifestation of contemporary community policing in England and Wales, participation is vital in meeting the needs and policing aims of the community. This is obtained in different ways, via informal and formal routes. Citizen-focused policing is defined as a way of working whereby an in-depth understanding of the needs and expectations of individuals and communities is routinely reflected in decision making, service delivery and practice (Home Office, 2006a; 2006b). This approach places the citizen at the centre of policing activity, and is thought to be a major contributing factor to the support of neighbourhood policing approaches.

Mastrofski (1999) identifies the six founding principles of citizen-focused policing, namely attentiveness, reliability, responsiveness, competence, manners and fairness. Mastrofski further highlights the lack of understanding that appears to exist within the police organisation of exactly what citizen-focused policing entails, with the police generally responding to its introduction by adding to already-existing practices, rather than embracing it as a new form of policing that is delivered by everyone. In addition, O'Neill (2014a) points out that engaging with communities in an effective manner is generally not well regarded within nor rewarded by the police organisation, as it does not fit in with the preferred (and possibly cultural) belief that policing is enforcement work only. For citizen-focused policing to become a core function, the police organisation needs to understand and accept the approach and also ensure that all staff in the organisation are fully involved in the process of change. Further, the organisation must ensure that its representatives provide communities with the best possible information regarding crime and disorder problems and how the police and partners are dealing with them, as well as providing proactive community engagement that is used to meet different and diverse community groups.

To try to understand how we have reached the current position in terms of pluralised policing in England and Wales, it is necessary to consider the historical context of this kind of approach. In December 2001, HMIC published a thematic inspection report entitled *Open All Hours: A Thematic Inspection Report on the Role of Police Visibility and Accessibility in Public Reassurance*. This report (HMIC, 2001) highlighted that, although the then British Crime Survey showed that crime had been reducing year on year since 1995, public opinion surveys demonstrated that fear of crime was increasing. To try to narrow this perceived gap, the report therefore suggested that the police service should attempt to become more visible, accessible and familiar with communities and to carry out their functions in a more 'community-focused style'. For the purposes of this report, the following definitions applied:

- Visibility referred to the level, profile and impact of police resources deployed within local communities.
- Accessibility meant the ease with which the public could obtain appropriate police information, access services or make contact with staff.
- Familiarity meant the extent to which police personnel both knew and were known by the local community.

The findings of this inspection became the catalyst for the National Reassurance Policing Programme and later the National Neighbourhood Policing Programme.

Eight police forces at 16 sites took part in the National Reassurance Policing Programme between 2003 and 2005. A key element of the programme was community engagement, which identified those issues seen as a priority for the local community. The requirement for local officers to be visible, accessible and familiar to community members was an integral part of the engagement process and of the community-focused style of policing advocated by the programme.

Early evaluation of the programme appeared to provide positive indicators in relation to public confidence in the local police and an increase in public reassurance. This led to the evolution of the National Neighbourhood Policing Programme.

National Neighbourhood Policing Programme

In November 2004, the government White Paper, entitled *Building Communities, Beating Crime: A Better Police Service for the 21st Century* (Home Office, 2004), laid the foundation for neighbourhood policing in England and Wales (enacted in amendments to the Police Reform Act 2002 in 2005). While the paper contained 10 main areas of commitment, perhaps the most pertinent were the second and sixth, which stated that citizens should:

- Know who their local police officer, community support officer and wardens are – and who is in charge – and how they can be contacted.

- Be clear about the roles which the police and other partners play in tackling anti-social behaviour and crime in communities and how they can be held to account – but also have the opportunity to have a real say in how their local communities are policed, with the confidence that their views will be listened to and acted upon. (Home Office, 2004, p 23)

Clearly the government believed that neighbourhood policing was the vehicle that could deliver on this commitment. As a result, all forces in England and Wales were required to implement neighbourhood policing by April 2008. In essence, there were three distinct requirements for neighbourhood policing. These were as follows:

- The consistent presence of dedicated neighbourhood teams capable of working with the community to establish and maintain control, to be visible, accessible, skilled, knowledgeable and familiar to the community.
- Intelligence-led identification of community concerns and prompt, effective, targeted action against those concerns.
- Joint action and problem solving with the community and other local partners to improve the local environment and quality of life within communities.

Prior to the November 2004 White Paper on neighbourhood policing, to the Police Reform Act 2002 (Home Office, 2002) was considered to be one of the most important Acts of Parliament regarding the police and policing in England and Wales in modern times. It formed the backbone of the government's agenda for reforming the police service in England and Wales and received Royal Assent on 24 July 2002. The provisions of the Act were brought about in stages by a series of Commencement Orders, thus allowing the government to implement certain parts of the Act when it saw fit. Perhaps one of the most influential aspects of this Act was the introduction of the police community support officer role.

Police community support officers

The Police Reform Act 2002 enabled chief police officers to introduce police community support officers (PCSOs), investigating officers, and detention and escort officers, to act as police authority support staff and to assist police officers in dealing with low-level crime and antisocial behaviour. This move was initially proposed in *Policing a New Century: A Blueprint for Reform* (Home Office, 2001) and had three main functions:

- Freeing up officers' time for core functions such as dealing with volume crime, thereby ensuring a more effective use of these individuals.
- Employing more specialist investigating officers to provide expertise in combating specialist crime in areas such as finance and information technology.
- Providing additional capacity to combat low-level disorder, and thereby help reduce the public's fear of crime. In this way, the government proposed to harness the commitment of those already engaged in crime reduction activities such as traffic wardens, neighbourhood and street wardens, and security staff.

The national PCSO website, which informs potential applicants of the role and work of PCSOs, seems quite clear regarding the requirements of the post, and it is worth considering this at some length to inform the context of this research.

> Police Community Support Officers are members of support staff, employed, directed and managed by their Police Force. They will work to complement and support regular police officers, providing a visible and accessible uniformed presence to improve the quality of life in the community and offer greater public reassurance. PCSOs are not replacement police officers but are there to address some of the tasks that do not require the experience or powers held by police officers, which often take officers away from more appropriate duties.
>
> Their primary purpose is to improve the community and offer greater public reassurance. In support of regular police officers they will work within a targeted patrol area to provide a visible and accessible uniformed presence; work with partners and community organisations to address anti-social behaviour, the fear of crime, environmental issues and other factors which affect the quality of people's lives. For example, reporting vandalism or damaged street furniture, reporting suspicious activity, providing crime prevention advice, deterring juvenile nuisance and visiting victims of crime. (PCSO, 2014)

Even though the Police Reform Act 2002 (Home Office, 2002) allows for great discretion regarding the powers granted to PCSOs within their force areas, the basic fundamental reason for the introduction of such a role within the police service remains the same: that of public reassurance, responding to street crime and disorder and engaging with citizens to obtain information.

Accreditation

The Police Reform Act 2002 introduces the ability to accredit members of the extended policing family such as street wardens. This means under certain circumstances, limited police powers can be granted to persons already engaged in community safety activities. It could also include individuals such as football stewards, as well as security guards within the private security industry. Even those with official powers, such as environmental health officers, may be included. Each relevant chief officer has discretion for conferring powers on accredited individuals, and they may also attach conditions and restrictions to the powers. Schedule 5 to the Police Reform Act 2002 lists a menu of powers that may be conferred on accredited individuals. These are as follows:

- Power to issue fixed penalty notices.
- Power to require giving of name and address.
- Power to require name and address of a person acting in an antisocial manner.
- Power to prevent alcohol consumption in designated public places.
- Power to confiscate alcohol and tobacco.
- Power to remove abandoned vehicles.

The idea of promoting community agencies, groups and individuals in an attempt to encourage social interaction and thus produce a more cohesive society is not particularly new. Previous official documents such as Wedlock's work on social cohesion (Home Office, 2006c), which promoted crime-resistant communities, have urged crime and disorder partnerships to engage in these types of activities. Further, the importance of social capital has been explored in the work of Robert Putnam, who considers the rise of criminal activity against a backcloth of social disengagement in the US (Putnam, 2000). Recent government ideas that extend this approach have been and are still being promoted by Halpern (2007; 2010), who served as an aide in the previous Labour government and later advised the Conservative–Liberal Democrat coalition government.

Aside from any social cohesive support neighbourhood policing teams may engender, from a practical point of view they also act as a conduit for information from communities to the police, which allows for a more efficient process of working. This is especially useful in terms of targeting scarce resources to particular problems. The use of community intelligence has been defined as:

> Local information which, when assessed, provides intelligence on issues that affect neighbourhoods and informs both the strategic and operational perspectives in the policing of local communities. Information may be direct and indirect and come from a diverse range of sources including the community and partner agencies. (ACPO, 2005, p 12)

Community intelligence is very important as it feeds into the process of intelligence-led policing. It should never be underestimated, as not only will it address policing issues from a general quality-of-life perspective, but it can also be used to address serious crime and, of course, terrorism. Effective local arrangements to capture this vital information are normally put in place and the success of neighbourhood policing depends on them in part. The importance of the role of information and intelligence gathering to policing is vital to understand. This is particularly so if in the future, different types of agencies, both public and private, have to work together to provide a system that is understandable and accountable.

National Intelligence Model

The National Intelligence Model (NIM) is a major introduction in the context of police reform. NIM is a model that ensures information is fully researched and analysed to provide intelligence that senior police managers can use to inform strategic direction, and to help them make tactical decisions about resourcing, operational policing and managing risk. One important point to note is that the model is not just about intelligence, but can be used for most areas of policing. For example, it sets the requirements for the contribution of patrolling, reactive, proactive and intelligence staff. When first introduced, it was viewed as a rational way in which policing should be delivered.

The Model has real value in that it clearly outlines the component parts of the intelligence process and clarifies terminology which is all too often misunderstood. Adoption of the model throughout the UK will ensure commonality in working practices and an understanding of the intelligence requirements which will ensure greater effectiveness in the future. (NCIS, 2000)

In essence, NIM is a business process. The intention behind it was to provide a focus on operational policing and to achieve a disproportionately greater impact from the resources applied to any problem. It is dependent on a clear framework of analysis of information and intelligence, allowing a problem-solving approach to law enforcement and crime prevention. The expected outcomes are improved community safety, reduced crime, and the control of criminality and disorder, leading to greater public reassurance and confidence.

The NIM was the product of work carried out by the National Criminal Intelligence Service on behalf of ACPO's Crime Committee at the time. It was envisaged that a more vigorous approach could be introduced into the management decision-making process for both strategic and tactical purposes. Its introduction, it was believed, would greatly help 'joined-up' law enforcement, and it would lose none of its initial impact when placed within a new pluralised policing approach.

The model was designed to have an impact at three levels of police activity, namely levels 1, 2, and 3. These levels are explained in Box 4.1.

Box 4.1: The components of NIM

Level 1: Daily tasking – local issues comprising the crimes, criminals, and other problems affecting a BCU. This area encompasses a wide range of matters from low-level theft to murder, and it is anticipated that the handling of volume crime will be at this level.

Level 2: Force/regional-level tasking – cross-border issues that affect more than one BCU. These may include problems that affect a group of BCUs or neighbouring forces, and may also involve support from other national agencies.

Level 3: National tasking – serious and organised crime that usually operates on a national and international scale will be dealt with at this level.

How NIM works

While the NIM is firstly a business model used to allocate police resources, there is a strong link between it and partnership working. An integral component of the model is information; all partners will be encouraged to provide as much information as possible at the beginning of the process, and to accept results following research and analysis so that they can be better informed about tactical or strategic issues.

However, much of the intelligence that is produced by NIM at the tactical level may be restricted or confidential and will often include names of targets and offenders. Users of NIM should be aware that there are a number of readily identifiable sources of information. These include victims, witnesses, offenders and informants. It is therefore essential that police officers, and in the future other members of the pluralised policing provision, gather information and intelligence from all sources and that it is processed through the intelligence systems in place. However, the question remains regarding the nature of restrictions in terms of information exchange between public, private and volunteer groups working together at a local level.

Currently, in terms of local partnerships, the Tactical Tasking and Coordinating Group comprises a chairperson and a small group of senior managers who have responsibility for one BCU and can make resourcing decisions. Part of their function is also to consider corporate intelligence products that may affect their local area as well as being represented at force level.

The neighbourhood team process is, in many respects, reliant on information and intelligence in a two-way flow between the team and the community. The introduction of more agencies and groups involved in the delivery of local, pluralised policing, however, means that the current structure for the gathering and management of information will need to be carefully considered.

An initial model of plural policing

As indicated previously, the concept of plural policing in England and Wales is perhaps most easily understood in the historical context of the approach of neighbourhood policing teams. Neighbourhood team policing appears quite straightforward. It is about dealing with crime and disorder more intelligently and building new relationships between the police and the public. This relationship should be one built on cooperation rather than mere consent. It relies on local people being part of the solution to local problems of crime and disorder. However, there are several other facets to neighbourhood team policing, and these are examined below.

First we need to understand what the phrase 'neighbourhood' means. The answer is that for the purposes of neighbourhood policing teams, its definition depends on many factors. These include:

• crime statistics;
• housing information; and
• employment information.

Many other social factors may define a 'neighbourhood'; for the police, therefore, neighbourhood cannot be viewed as just a political ward or group of houses. To a person living in the inner city, the idea of 'neighbourhood' may seem different from that of someone living in a country village. A whole council may appear to be a neighbourhood in one instance, while in some areas it can mean a political ward.

The government, in pursuing neighbourhood policing, suggested that the definition of 'neighbourhood' should be decided by local communities, police forces and authorities and their partners rather than being defined by the government itself. What comprises a neighbourhood for policing teams will therefore vary across the country. Now that we realise that the definition of a 'neighbourhood' is not quite as simple as we thought, we need to consider just what a neighbourhood policing team appears to constitute. The way the team operates, in theory, can be seen in Figure 4.1.

Figure 4.1: Theoretical representation of typical neighbourhood policing team

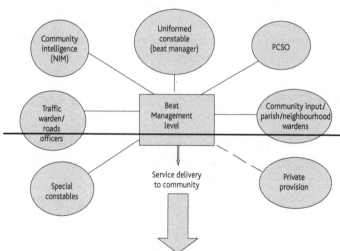

According to this theoretical model, all partners appear to have an equal input to the process of delivering policing services based on information and intelligence for that area. It is the police constable who is envisaged as being the facilitator or beat manager, ensuring that policing is delivered where it is needed, as well as providing the desired reassurance through targeted high-visibility patrol.

The idea of neighbourhood policing teams tackling crime and antisocial behaviour is now a well-established one. A good example of this from Merseyside and Leicester can be seen in the Box 4.2 below.

Box 4.2: The implementation of NPTs in Merseyside and Leicester

Merseyside Police have split the area into 43 'neighbourhoods', which equates to two or three council wards per neighbourhood. Teams are headed by an inspector, who has responsibility for a number of sergeants and constables, supported by PCSOs, special constables and volunteers. In consultation with the community, the teams tackle issues that really affect people. Local surveys indicate that crime has been reduced and public satisfaction increased since their introduction.

In Leicester, officers are given small areas or 'micro-beats' to patrol and oversee. These can be a small number of streets, an estate or a hotspot. Officers are considered guardians of their area, solving problems and listening to local people. In one area alone, crime has fallen by 20 per cent as a result of this initiative.

This approach should, of course, be much more than just high-visibility reassurance policing. It uses local knowledge and intelligence from local people to target crime hotspots and disorder issues causing most concern to local communities. The previous government stated that teams would be supported by the latest technology, and initiatives included issuing mobile telephone numbers to individuals within neighbourhoods to enable them to contact the local beat manager directly.

Neighbourhood policing teams would mean that people:

- *knew who their local police officers* were and how to contact them;
- had a *real say in local policing* issues and setting local priorities;
- *knew how well their police were doing* locally in tackling crime and antisocial behaviour.

Neighbourhood teams are seen as an excellent example of delivering police services through a variety of different people, not just sworn police officers. The people engaged in this activity are often referred to as the extended policing family, and illustrate the point that plural policing is not necessarily a very recent approach.

The extended policing family

We have seen how the introduction of the Police Reform Act 2002 (Home Office, 2002) led to substantial change in the police service, and it is the same Act that enables us, with some accuracy, to help predict the future delivery of policing. The introduction of PCSOs, coupled with the use of neighbourhood watch and local warden schemes, resulted in a more flexible method for dealing with community problems, even if these unsworn officers lacked sufficient powers to carry out their role fully. This is because it is the chief officer of police in the area where they are employed who decides what powers they are allowed to hold, in line with those outlined in the Police Reform Act 2002. With this in mind, the theoretical extended police family, responsible for day-to-day policing of crime and disorder, is worthy of brief exploration. While not all of the roles discussed here are directly involved in day-to-day policing as part of the NPT approach, their presence and input at various times has contributed to the success of the approach.

Uniformed constable

The role of the uniformed constable is considered crucial to coordinating service delivery. This enables the constable to perform a more proactive role in consultation, coordinating delivery through the various officers available, and where necessary using the full powers of a police constable. The role of constable dramatically alters from that of law enforcer to facilitator and leader. However, recent austerity measures combined with reductions to the police budget suggest that this role will be much more difficult to perform as greater demands are placed on constables' time.

Police specials

The powers invested in police specials, who are volunteers, are exactly the same as for regular officers (Bullock, 2014). In theory at least, specials receive the same level of training as regular officers, wear the same uniforms, and provide invaluable support in many situations. As volunteers, they are able to offer only a certain amount of their time. Despite this, and if their availability is intelligently managed, they can provide useful high-visibility patrol, backed up with the lawful authority to use force if necessary, just like sworn police officers. This important role is discussed more fully in Chapter Six.

Police community support officers

PCSOs, working with other members of the delivery team, not only to provide reassurance through visible patrolling at relevant times, but also resolve low-level community problems through the use of their powers to do so (Crawford et al, 2005). They provide the beat manager with invaluable assistance in dealing with minor instances of public disorder and antisocial problems. Chapter Five explores in more detail their role and contribution to recent and future policing.

Traffic wardens

The role of traffic warden became a constituent part of the theory of neighbourhood policing teams with the idea that wardens could be used not only to enforce road traffic offences but also to issue fixed-penalty notices for certain other offences. They were capable of obtaining information for the policing team, and could supply criminal and community intelligence through their visible presence on the street. They were available to deal with local traffic problems as well as being involved in maintaining safety on the roads, albeit their actual role in the neighbourhood policing team approach could be contested. However, the role of the traffic warden in this context has diminished considerably in recent years to the extent that it practically no longer exists.

Parish or neighbourhood wardens

Originally conceived as an 'eyes and ears' approach for the police, coupled with concierge and reassurance functions, warden schemes could be used as a means of issuing fixed penalties for various offences such as minor criminal damage (graffiti) or littering. The increase in surveillance and reassurance provided by high-visibility patrolling would have been an invaluable asset to the beat manager. It was the introduction of PCSOs under the Police Reform Act 2002 that eventually saw the demise of much of this type of provision.

Private security provision

It was entirely possible that private security officers could be used within neighbourhood teams to enhance policing capability. While the main function of the private security industry was originally the protection of private property, there has been an increase in their use for such roles as prisoner escort, as well as other custodial duties assisting sworn officers. The Private Security Industry Act 2001, which regulates the industry, had wide repercussions for the use of private security in the public domain of policing. The main areas of activity now include wheel clamping, the guarding of premises and the provision of security consultant services. Section 40 of the Police Reform Act 2002 introduced the Community Safety Accreditation Scheme, which was designed to extend limited police powers to persons already engaged in community safety duties. These include local authority wardens as well as security guards within private security industry. However, it appears that the use of private security within neighbourhood teams has never been a major feature of such initiatives. Private policing provision is discussed elsewhere in this book.

Volunteers

A clear theme of the current government agenda for reform and modernisation of public services is the development of new ways of involving local communities in shaping the priorities and outputs of public service delivery. This involves identifying new and less formalised methods of communication between public services and service users to make delivery of services more responsive to the needs of local people. Generally speaking, the police service in England and Wales has a modest record in the involvement of volunteers in its activities. The special constabulary has been the principal initiative and significant effort has been put into recruitment, retention and empirical evaluation of the business and community benefits of using these volunteers. Police volunteers (see Bullock, 2014) in their various guises are discussed in greater depth elsewhere in this book.

Modern approaches to the NPT concept

The most recent Labour government, in office until 2010, was fully supportive of the NPT and citizen-involved policing approach. In 2008, for example, the Home Office (2008) introduced a policing pledge that promised to:

- ensure that 80 per cent of duty time was spent within the neighbourhood area and that officers were visible on patrol where they were needed;
- publish details of each NPT; and
- reduce staff turnover, to improve consistency of contact with local officers.

This document also included one numerical target for the police – that of improving public confidence. However, this pledge was removed with the change of government in 2010 as a way of freeing the police and other agencies from what was seen as 'top-down' centralised control, while also preparing the organisation for dealing with large reductions in its funding. In 2010, the Home Office published a consultation paper (Home Office, 2010a), which included major reform proposals with important implications for the future resourcing and operation of neighbourhood policing, namely the introduction of Police and Crime Commissioners (PCCs).

This role replaced the old tripartite system of accountability in England and Wales, which was considered unfit for purpose in a modern accountable society. The PCC role was introduced in 2012 with the aim of making policing more democratic and locally accountable. PCCs were to have a statutory duty to consult members of the public regarding which issues the police should prioritise and to include these within their police and crime plans.

However, perhaps the most influential change to have affected the delivery of NPTs is that of the large reduction to policing budgets. Following a long period during which officer numbers increased, the number of full-time equivalent officers in England and Wales has fallen by 11 per cent since 2010 – roughly 16,000 officers. In 2013, HMIC warned that neighbourhood policing was the area of policing most at risk in terms of cuts (HMIC, 2013) and highlighted concerns over the numbers of PCSOs, for whom the planned reduction between March 2010 and March 2015 was 22 per cent. In particular, both the Independent Police Commission (2013) and the Police Federation (2014) have raised concerns about the impact of these cuts on neighbourhood policing, the latter resulting in a charge of scaremongering by the Home Secretary, Theresa May, May, 2014). The Police Federation survey (2014) suggested that 33 of the 43 forces in England and Wales have scrapped, reduced or merged their neighbourhood policing teams since 2010. Moreover, many chief constables have been trying to recruit more and more volunteer special constables, while in Leicestershire, remaining neighbourhood officers will no longer investigate crimes or respond to emergencies, but deal only with core community activities such as patrolling and engaging with people.

It is anticipated that further cuts to police resources will continue at least for the foreseeable future, with police forces continuing to receive demands to deliver high-quality services, including neighbourhood policing. The challenges for the future of neighbourhood policing include the following:

- working effectively across local, regional and national borders;
- responding to new kinds of offences such as cyber-crime;
- engaging with increasingly transient and diverse communities and with citizens connected through social media;
- meeting increasing public expectations for security and the demand for a visible presence.

A new model of NPT policing?

It is well established that the role of the neighbourhood policing team has been fundamental to the community policing approach in England and Wales. How then will the drive for a more pluralised approach affect the delivery of such an important facet of policing? Recent times have seen the removal of the role of the traffic warden and an increase in private policing provision. The attempt to increase the number of volunteers for policing activities has gained momentum through the government's 'Big Society' approach, as well as the drive for police volunteers. The reduction in the number of police officers (Home Office, 2015) can only lead to speculation regarding how involved the public police will actually become in the delivery of local policing. It may be that the public police will only have limited control or input, being called into communities as and when they are required. Figure 4.2 illustrates a possible new approach to NPT with a much-reduced public police input.

Clearly, there is an anticipated rise in the use of other agencies, including private provision as well as vastly increased citizen and community input into the policing of communities. Whether this is possible remains to be seen. The danger for the public police in this new era of austerity has been highlighted by the HMIC 2014), which has pointed out that the police service may retreat to reactive, response-oriented policing, with resources being deployed to respond to immediate demands rather than more strategic long-term issues. Engaging with communities, neighbourhood policing and partnership working may all be at risk as other publicly owned agencies, under the same austerity measures as the police, retreat towards what is considered their core functions. Thus, we may see a decrease in proactive, crime prevention activities undertaken by NPTs, which could ultimately lead to more reactive policing responses and a spiralling demand for a higher standard of service in policing.

Figure 4.2: Possible new structure for NPTs

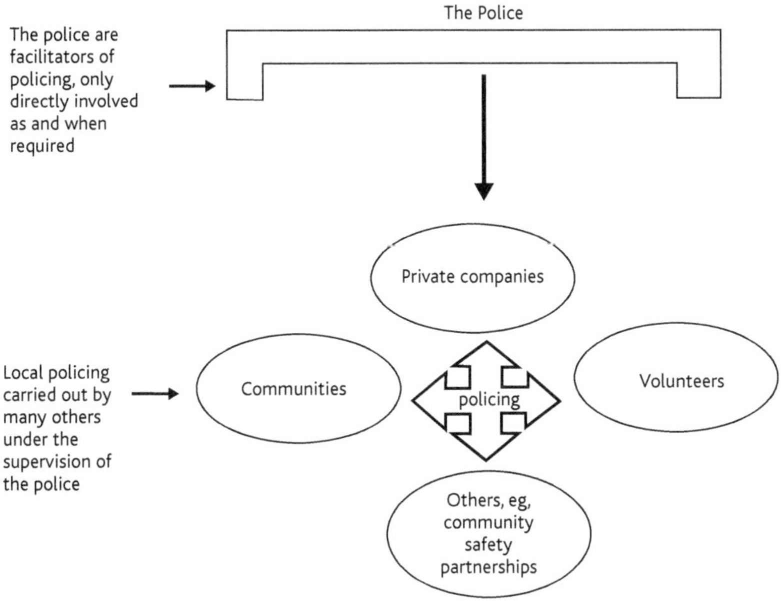

The Police

The police are facilitators of policing, only directly involved as and when required

Local policing carried out by many others under the supervision of the police

Private companies

Communities

policing

Volunteers

Others, eg, community safety partnerships

Conclusion

We have seen that the idea of multi-agency, local-level policing is not a particularly new one; the concept of neighbourhood policing as a plural policing approach was a sound one that appears to have had a major impact on public reassurance and crime reduction. However, austerity measures, coupled with a change in political viewpoints, seems to have heralded the decline of such an approach. Yet even a cursory view of the NPT approach illustrates that there are areas that will need deeper consideration should there be an increase in the use of private security and other forms of provision and a further decline in public police numbers. Questions revolve around the complex areas of police legitimacy and accountability as well as information exchange.

The examination of the NPT approach affords us an opportunity for greater understanding of a plural policing approach for the future.

Further reading

ACPO (2006) *Practice Advice on Professionalising the Business of Neighbourhood Policing*, Wyboston: Centrex.

Bullock, K. and Sindall, K. (2014) 'Examining the nature and extent of public participation in neighbourhood policing', *Policing and Society*, vol 24, no 44, pp 385-404.

Crawford, A. and Lister, S. (2004) *The extended policing family: Visible patrols in residential areas*, Joseph Rowntree Foundation.

Fielding, N. (2009) *Getting the best out of community policing*. Police Foundation.

Flanagan, R. (2008) *Lancashire Constabulary: Neighbourhood Policing Developing Citizen Focused Policing*, London: Central Office of Information.

HMIC (Her Majesty's Inspectorate of Constabulary) (2014) *Policing in Austerity: Meeting the challenge*, available at https://www.justiceinspectorates.gov.uk/hmic/wp-content/uploads/policing-in-austerity-meeting-the-challenge.pdf

Home Office (2001) *Policing a New Century: A Blueprint for Reform*, London, Home Office.

Morash, M. and Ford, J.K. (eds) (2002) *The move to community policing: Making change happen*, Sage Publications.

O'Neill, M. (2014a) 'Ripe for the chop or the public face of policing? PCSOs and neighbourhood policing in austerity', *Policing*, vol 8, no 3, pp 265-73.

O'Neill, M. (2014b) 'Playing nicely with others', in J.M. Brown (ed) *The Future of Policing*, Abingdon: Routledge.

Savage, S. (2007) *Police reform: forces for change*, Oxford: Oxford University Press.

Skogan, W. (1990) *Disorder and Decline: Crime and the Spiral of Decay in American Neighbourhoods*, New York, NY: Free Press.

Trojanowicz, R.C. (1983) *An Evaluation of the Neighbourhood Foot Patrol Program in Flint, Michigan*, East Lansing, MI: Michigan State University Press.

FIVE

Police community support officers

Introduction

This chapter critically evaluates the introduction of police community support officers (PCSOs), and considers their complementary role alongside sworn officers. It could be argued that the introduction of PCSOs was a means for the police organisation to manage an inevitable drift towards plural policing, by having control over a resource that consisted of 'non-sworn' staff. The chapter discusses the contribution of PCSOs to social capital and crime prevention, as well as how the police occupational sub-culture has reacted to such a change in the delivery of policing. It will also include a critical discussion of the proposal to enhance the role of the PCSOs, which would mean allowing them to utilise enhanced police powers as witnessed within some police forces as they try to deliver a level of service under difficult economic circumstances.

PCSOs are believed to have played a major part in increasing engagement and interaction with local communities. PCSOs were first introduced in 2002, but initially both the public and the police service appeared sceptical. Although their primary role was to contribute to public reassurance through visibility and accessibility as part of the neighbourhood policing team approach and the reassurance programme, there was confusion at first as to what this entailed. A national evaluation of the role in 2004 identified a range of non-standard tasks being undertaken by PCSOs, which included distributing crime prevention advice, collecting evidence for Anti-Social Behaviour Orders, conducting minor house-to-house enquiries and providing witness support (Cooper et al, 2006). Concerns arose that the PCSO role, with limited powers compared with those of a police officer, would become simply a cheap way to fulfil some officer functions (Caless, 2007).

PCSOs today

PCSOs are now recognised as a useful addition to the policing family (O'Neill, 2015). Given the depth of local knowledge that PCSOs can acquire from their beat areas, they can help to address problems in a neighbourhood and gather intelligence for police colleagues, ultimately playing a key role in improving police legitimacy with the public (Foster and Jones, 2010) . PCSOs are seen as skilled at negotiation and discussion (O'Neill, 2015) and are more ethnically diverse than police officers or staff; 9.1 per cent black and minority ethnic staff work as PCSOs compared with 5.5 per cent of officers and 6.9 per cent of other police staff respectively (Cooper et al, 2006). Evidence shows that neighbourhood policing, particularly through the use of PCSOs, has had a significant impact on the way the police engage with diverse communities (O'Neill, 2015). The national evaluation of PCSOs undertaken by the Home Office in 2006 demonstrated that they were particularly valued for their work in tackling local problems involving young people, and engaging with and reassuring the public (Cooper et al, 2006). However, PCSOs are police staff and are not warranted officers, so they can more easily be made redundant. Indeed, in the past few years their numbers have fallen (Home Office, 2015a), although most police forces are maintaining the same proportion of PCSOs in their operational workforce. Recent research suggests that a decrease in the number of PCSOs results in the impairment of neighbourhood policing, while increasing their number comparably enhances it (Greig-Midlane, 2014). Having said this, there is also evidence to suggest that their role is changing. A 2014 report by Her Majesty's Inspectorate of Constabulary (HMIC) found that PCSOs were taking on more roles and responsibilities, some of which removed them from community engagement, such as guarding crime scenes, enforcing road closures, detaining suspects or young people, giving out fixed penalty notices and responding to low-level emergencies (HMIC, 2014). Some forces have found new sources of funding for PCSOs, such as through local authorities. Telford and Wrekin, for example, are subsidising the cost of PCSOs while allowing the local council to have some influence over daily tasking (Police Foundation, 2014). Some forces have suggested that it is helpful to divide activities into those that could be done by unsworn staff and those that specifically require a police response. So, for example, offering advice to burglary victims could be given by a range of people (aided by the police), whereas dealing with a major public disorder incident can only be done by a warranted officer (Police Foundation, 2014). There is a range of activities that can be undertaken by people other than sworn police officers, and this is an important facet of plural policing. In order to fully understand and critically evaluate their role thus far, however, it is useful to consider the background to the introduction of PCSOs.

Historical context

The level of crime in England and Wales, as measured by the British Crime Survey (BCS), has fallen consistently since a peak in 1995. The risk of becoming a victim of crime has fallen from 40 per cent in 1995 to 26 per cent in 2003/04, the lowest level recorded since the BCS began in 1981. However, at the same time, two thirds (65 per cent) of the public believed that crime in the country as a whole had increased in the previous two years, with a third thinking it had risen 'a lot 'in the 2003/04 survey (Dodd et al, 2004).

The thematic inspection report *Open All Hours*, compiled by HMIC, explored this disparity between success in crime reduction and the apparent lack of an equivalent impact on the public's confidence in the police and perceptions of crime, and identified a 'reassurance gap' (HMIC, 2001). When asked in surveys what would improve their feelings of safety, satisfaction and confidence in the police, members of the public have consistently highlighted a desire for greater levels of foot patrol. However, the role of the police officer has changed in recent years, resulting in less time being spent on the beat. An examination of how officers' time was spent (PA Consulting Group, 2001) confirmed that most time outside the station was spent responding to incidents and making enquiries, and that most officer patrol was carried out in cars. In addition, many activities keep police officers off the beat; making an arrest, for example, could keep an officer in the station for three-and-a-half hours. There appeared to be a gap between the public desire for visible patrol and the ability of the police service to provide that function. Consequently, the issue of how to reassure the public was high on the agenda at this time. PCSOs were introduced as a way of increasing the visible presence of the police organisation through patrol on foot. In relation to improving perceived police effectiveness and increasing feelings and perceptions of safety, the mechanisms of increasing police visibility and familiarity and the increased levels of foot patrol were found to be most effective (Dalgleish and Myhill, 2004).

The government at this time had made a commitment to deliver neighbourhood policing to all communities. The aim was to 'make communities feel safe and secure by reducing crime and anti-social behaviour in their area' (Home Office, 2005b), through the work of visible and accessible neighbourhood policing teams that were responsive to local priorities. The successful implementation of neighbourhood policing involved engaging the public and using local intelligence to target deployment of the teams. PCSOs were to have a key part to play in the local mixed teams that included officers, special constables, wardens and others and constituted a new form of plural policing.

The introduction of PCSOs through the Police Reform Act 2002 represented a fundamental change in policing. The Act extended the role of police staff (personnel employed by a police organisation who do not have the sworn status of a constable) to assist sworn police officers and carry out many front-line roles, giving authority to the chief officer of a police force to designate any person who is employed by the police authority as a PCSO and confer on that person any of a list of powers given in the Act. This list was subsequently expanded through later legislation. In particular, PCSOs were intended to provide a visible, uniformed patrolling presence and tackle antisocial behaviour. In order to assist with the introduction of PCSOs, Home Office funds were made available from 2002 onwards and implementation of the PCSO initiative was rapid.

The total number of PCSOs currently employed in England and Wales can be seen in Table 5.1.

The current situation regarding PCSOs can be summarised using data provided by the Home Office (2015b). According to the latest report, the number of PCSOs fell between 31 March 2014 and 31 March 2015 by 5 per cent or 735 PCSOs, out of a national total of 11,719 staff available for duty. Within this figure, 45 per cent of PCSOs were female and 55 per cent male. Between March 2006 and March 2010, the numbers of PCSOs generally increased, but since that time a discernible trend of reduction of PCSOs can be observed, perhaps reflecting wider government policy in terms of policing within England and Wales. Currently, PCSOs constitute 6 per cent of the total police workforce.

Table 5.1: Number of PCSOs by force in England and Wales, March 2015

England and Wales						
	Total			Minority ethnic		
	Male	Female	Total	Male	Female	Total
Avon & Somerset	157	174	331	15	3	18
Bedfordshire	55	50	105	6	4	10
Cambridgeshire	72	76	148	9	6	15
Cheshire	123	102	225	1	2	3
Cleveland	80	43	123	0	0	0
Cumbria	35	51	86	1	0	1
Derbyshire	84	79	163	4	8	12
Devon & Cornwall	193	153	346	2	1	3
Dorset	100	63	163	1	0	1
Durham	87	70	157	1	1	2
Essex	109	153	262	3	3	6
Gloucestershire	62	66	128	3	1	4
Greater Manchester	492	313	804	68	20	87
Hampshire	148	153	302	5	3	8
Hertfordshire	110	100	210	9	5	14
Humberside	139	135	273	4	1	5
Kent	187	165	352	3	5	8
Lancashire	169	162	331	13	1	14
Leicestershire	142	92	234	21	3	24
Lincolnshire	66	72	138	3	0	3
London, City of	10	1	11	4	0	4
Merseyside	192	161	353	4	5	9
Metropolitan Police	1,145	642	1,787	489	152	642
Norfolk	112	86	197	1	1	2
Northamptonshire	74	48	122	5	1	6
Northumbria	129	82	211	2	2	4
North Yorkshire	108	88	196	0	1	1
Nottinghamshire	172	146	318	9	1	10
South Yorkshire	185	130	314	10	5	15
Staffordshire	105	104	208	4	4	8
Suffolk	97	70	167	1	1	2
Surrey	62	61	123	3	2	5
Sussex	144	181	325	3	4	7
Thames Valley	233	226	459	20	9	29

England and Wales						
	Total			Minority ethnic		
	Male	Female	Total	Male	Female	Total
Warwickshire	35	51	86	3	3	6
West Mercia	108	100	209	3	3	6
West Midlands	327	293	620	42	32	74
West Yorkshire	362	263	625	27	5	32
Wiltshire	59	70	129	4	0	4
Dyfed-Powys	75	72	147	1	0	1
Gwent	89	97	185	3	5	8
North Wales	122	121	243	2	2	4
South Wales	239	172	411	8	1	9
Total of all 43 forces	5,537	820	1,126			
British Transport Police	240	79	319	37	8	45
Total	7,033	5,616	12,649	857	314	1,171

Source: Home Office (2015).

Legislative powers

The statutory term for PCSO is community support officer, but to emphasise that they are under the control and direction of the police service and to distinguish them from other agencies' staff involved in community safety, they were soon invariably called police community support officers by police forces. As unsworn officers, PCSOs needed to have their powers enshrined by the Police Reform Act 2002 to enable them to carry out their role effectively. These are highlighted in the following section, and are considered under the section of the Act entitled 'Exercise of police powers etc. by civilians'.

As proposed in *Policing a New Century: A Blueprint for Reform* (Home Office, 2001), the Act provides for specified police support staff and civilians to be given particular powers in various defined circumstances in order to perform certain defined functions. The purpose of this was three-fold:

• First, it was intended to free up police officer time for their core functions by making more effective use of support staff, including detention officers, escort officers, and investigating officers acting as scenes of crime officers.

- Second, as part of the drive to tackle crime more effectively, it was the government's intention to enable forces to employ specialist investigating officers to provide expertise in combating specialist crime, in such areas as finance and information technology. The Act enabled such investigators to be granted the powers necessary to enable them to do their job effectively.
- Third, the Act was designed to provide additional capacity to combat low-level disorder, and thereby help reduce the public's fear of crime. The Act enabled chief officers to appoint suitable support staff (PCSOs) to roles providing a visible presence in the community, with powers sufficient to deal with minor issues. Such staff would be under the formal direction and control of the chief officer. The government also wanted to harness the commitment of those already involved in crime reduction activities, such as traffic wardens, neighbourhood and street wardens and security staff, as part of an extended police family. The Act made provision for community safety accreditation schemes and a railway safety accreditation scheme and, in certain circumstances, the granting of limited powers to accredited members of those schemes. In addition, there were several sections of the Act that laid down specific powers attributed to the role of the PCSO. The most important of these powers are illustrated in Table 5.2.

Clearly, the powers listed above indicate the street-level work envisaged for the community support officer, thus releasing sworn officers for other duties. PCSOs were to interact with a number of other agencies in performing those wider 'policing' duties. Despite claims that their introduction had been a success, PCSOs were not universally accepted as being a valuable addition to the policing family by all.

Reaction to PCSOs

Since their inception, PCSOs have been the target of unremitting criticism, including the accusation that they have replaced 'real' police officers, the suggestion that they are not suitably well trained to patrol neighbourhoods, and that they do not having sufficient powers to carry out their role properly (Caless, 2007). The Police Federation appears to have determined the way in which criticism of the introduction of PCSOs developed. Clearly, there was a fear that PCSOs were introduced to undermine the role of the constable. This fear was apparent in the words of the then national chair of the Police Federation, who informed the then Home Secretary in 2006

Table 5.2: Important powers for PCSOs

Relevant section of the Police Reform Act 2002	Specific powers and duties
Section 192	Lists powers and duties dealing with misconduct in public places, including the issue of fixed penalty notices (FPNs) for antisocial behaviour, litter and so on, and gives powers to request name and address from person(s) committing an offence that causes injury, alarm, distress or damage to another.
Section 195	Enables suitably designated persons to exercise powers to issue FPNs for a range of offences, including being drunk in a public highway, throwing fireworks, wasting police time, among many other antisocial behaviour and disorder offences.
Section 196	Sets out the power to require the name and address of a person believed to have committed an offence as designated. If the person fails to provide the name and address, or the information given is believed to be false, PCSOs can require that person to remain with them for up to 30 minutes pending the arrival of a constable. Alternatively, that person can freely accompany the PCSO to a police station rather than wait. Section 198 of the Act specifies the circumstances in which a PCSO may use reasonable force in the exercise of his powers to detain.
Sections 199 and 200	These sections outline powers for the confiscation of alcohol and the prevention of the consumption of alcohol in designated places.
Sections 204, 205 and 206	These sections relate to powers involving the use of vehicles, including the removal of abandoned vehicles, the power to stop and direct traffic and to carry out authorised road checks.
Section 207	This section enables the extension of strictly limited powers of a constable under the Terrorism Act 2000. The purpose of extending such powers to designated PCSOs is to enable them to provide valuable support to constables in times of terrorist threat, and to give chief officers the discretion to deploy constables for duties that require their full expertise and powers in such times. If specified in a PCSO's designation, paragraph 14 of this section confers on the officer the powers of a constable under section 36 of the Terrorism Act 2000 to enforce a cordoned area, where the cordoned area has been established under the Terrorism Act.

that PCSOs were an example of cheaper policing not better policing, despite government assurances that they would be supporting police officers and not replacing them (Berry et al, 1998). Perhaps these comments are understandable; the Federation was clearly arguing in defence of its members, and there did appear to be widespread unease that PCSOs represented a shift towards policing 'on the cheap', with the increase in PCSO numbers potentially threatening the recruitment of more police officers.

However, the wider changes affecting the police and policing in this country may have very little to do with the role of the PCSO directly. It may be that other changes, such as the rise of private policing in which many of the functions of the traditional police are being contracted out to private companies, security firms, or to people who perform patrol functions, will occur. The point the Federation appears to have missed is that policing was undergoing a profound change in England and Wales, and the introduction of PCSOs was merely one among many changes.

Jones (2008) highlights the fact that the Act of Parliament that launched PCSOs, the Police Reform Act 2002, also provided for the introduction of a national neighbourhood and street warden programme, which funded the growth of warden schemes throughout England and Wales. In general, warden schemes conducted local patrols, delivered public reassurance and undertook crime prevention activities.

When discussing the broad topic of civilianisation within the police in England and Wales, Neyroud (2010) suggests that the idea of PCSOs came from the Dutch *Stadswacht* scheme of the early 1990s, and was introduced to support the national reassurance policing programme. Civilianisation is the process by which fully attested, sworn police officers are replaced with civilian staff who have few or limited police powers, and who provide either administrative or specialist support to police. English and Welsh police forces were initially invited to bid for additional funds for the piloting of PCSOs. Following the initial evaluation of the pilot (see Cooper et al, 2006), the government committed itself to providing 24,000 PCSOs across the country. This target was subsequently reduced and by the spring of 2007, some 16,000 PCSOs were recruited and in place. The recruitment of PCSOs was rejected by the Police Federation, which viewed such officers as 'plastic' police. However, the national evaluation (Cooper et al, 2006) found generally strong support from communities, as had the earlier Dutch scheme. The public, it appeared, liked the fact that, unlike police officers, PCSOs were more rooted in the community, as were police officers. Despite this, critics pointed to the fact that there was some confusion among the public concerning the powers and role of PCSOs, and the failure to create an effective career structure for them has been problematic.

Johnston (2005) highlights the role the introduction of PCSOs has had on the diversity of the police service as a whole, believing that it will also have an impact on the diversity of sworn officers, as many of them tend to be recruited first as PCSOs. Indeed, in his work, some 47 per cent of PCSOs viewed their job as a stepping stone to the regular police, based on a survey of 2,025 PCSO recruit applications. This survey also considered the integration of PCSOs within wider policing team activities and concluded that this was slightly problematic; however, in areas where there was good supervision and planning, integration appeared to have occurred much more smoothly.

Evaluation of the role

Crawford (2008) regards the introduction of PCSOs into the police as the most momentous example of civilianisation that has been introduced in the history of the police service. For him, PCSOs are a new breed of patrol officer who provide a visible presence to combat low-level antisocial behaviour and give the public reassurance. They were intended to support constables and release them from tasks that do not require the level of skill, powers and training that constables possess. These not inconsiderable powers meant that the work of the PCSO was worthy of closer examination and drew an initial interest from researchers into their role.

Early research into the activities of PCSOs can be summarised in Table 5.3.

Table 5.3: Early research into activities of PCSOs

Taffin et al (2006)	Suggests PCSOs have had a significant positive impact on perceptions of crime and antisocial behaviour, feelings of safety and public confidence in the police.
Crawford et al (2004)	Questions the long-term reassurance value of PCSOs beyond the symbolic presence of uniformed police personnel.
Crawford et al (2005)	Highlights public concern regarding the role of PCSOs and the powers available to them.
Cooper et al (2006)	This national survey found variable implementation of the different powers available to PCSOs across the country.

In response to the apparent confusion around patterns of different powers, the government introduced a framework of standard powers by way of Statutory Instrument (SI 2007/3202), which came into force in December 2007. These powers relate largely to the use of fixed penalty notices for antisocial behaviour. However, there still remains a considerable list of additional (discretionary) powers from which chief constables can select.

The main success of PCSOs has been the support they have provided for facilitating the institutionalisation of neighbourhood policing teams across the country, in addition to the role they have played in helping to diversify the police in terms of ethnicity, gender and age.

Findings from the national evaluation of the introduction of PCSOs (Cooper et al, 2006) can be summarised as follows:

- PCSOs were seen as being more accessible than police officers. Members of the public were more likely to report things to PCSOs that they would not bother a police officer with, and to pass information on to them.
- The public valued the role of PCSOs and there was strong evidence from case studies in Manchester, Northumbria and Sussex to suggest that, where PCSOs were known in their communities, there was a perception that they had made a real impact in their areas, especially in dealing with youth disorders.
- The diversity of PCSOs, particularly in terms of ethnicity and age, had been a marked feature of the implementation.
- There was no evidence that PCSOs were having a measurable impact on the level of recorded crime or incidents of antisocial behaviour in areas where they were deployed.

However, the evaluation noted that this was early research into the impact of PCSOs, and conceded that it may be a little premature in some of its findings.

More recent research has tended to concentrate on the interaction between PCSOs and police officers as they perform their functions as part of a policing team. O'Neill (2015), utilising Goffman's dramaturgical model approach (1990) to the roles of PCSOs and police officers in this function, suggests in fact PCSOs and police constables comprise two separate teams. This has obvious implications for smooth service delivery to the public if both elements of the team operate separately. O'Neill's observational research further suggests that if PCSOs feel supported in their work, they are more likely to take an active interest in it, to pass on intelligence and provide a good service to the public. Cosgrove (2016), in her research into PCSOs and police occupational sub-culture, found that PCSOs dealt with the culture by demonstrating a certain amount of acquiescence, due in part to many PCSOs wanting to become police officers and in part to the absence of an internal career development path for them. She sees PCSOs as passive recipients of the traditional occupational culture but also being denied full membership of it by virtue of the fact that they are deemed 'outsiders' who play a limited role in the policing family.

In terms of public perceptions of the role of PCSOs, Rowland and Coupe's (2014) work at shopping malls in southern England suggest that police officers present high levels of reassurance while PCSOs emit notably weaker safety control signals than police constables, and evoke levels of safety reassurance that differ little from other non-police officers such as accredited safety officers or private security officers.

Conclusion

Clearly, PCSOs represent an attempt to maintain patrol function within the remit and control of the public police. Since the inception of the role, PCSOs have been the target of criticism (Caless, 2007). This has ranged from PCSOs being viewed as a cheap replacement for 'real' police officers, to them not being trained sufficiently for their role and possessing insufficient powers to compel compliance. They were awarded the title 'numpties' or 'blockheads' by the Police Federation during 2004, which is ironically reminiscent of the hostility displayed towards police officers as 'blue bottles', 'peelers' and 'blue locusts' following their introduction in the mid-19th century (Storch, 1975).

'Mission creep' has been highlighted as a perceived threat to the constable's role, but there are a large number of roles and other tasks now being done by unsworn officers, including custody work, crime scene investigation, fingerprinting and media relations, all of which have previously been undertaken by police officers. The apparent mission creep may also point to the fact that there may still be a consistent misunderstanding of the nature and scope of the work of PCSOs among some police managers. A key challenge for the future, therefore, is the extent to which PCSOs may become drawn into carrying out new tasks to fill service gaps, and/or become enforcement officers that engage with local communities in problem solving and crime prevention. There are signs that mission creep and incremental growth in the powers granted to PCSOs are becoming more evident, with the possibility of adverse implications for the reassurance role. In addition, PCSOs have provided a way for the police to compete in the security marketplace with private and other policing providers in a growing pluralised policing landscape.

Whether they remain in their present role and function is debateable, as austerity measures continue and further reduction in numbers of police officers seems inevitable. At the time of writing, the Home Office had launched a consultation process around some of the topics discussed in this chapter and we are awaiting the result. Of particular interest will be decisions surrounding the increase in the use of powers available to PCSOs.

Should the new neighbourhood policing team structure similar to that suggested in this work become a reality, it is hard to see how local policing provision could be effective without PCSOs (and possibly others) having sufficient powers to deal with day-to-day crime and antisocial behaviour.

In support of this approach, in 2015 the College of Policing conducted an analysis of demand on policing (College of Policing, 2015a). This analysis confirms that much of the work of the police revolves around public protection issues, and it is predicted that this will increase. Consequently, the College of Policing has attempted to upskill PCSOs for an increased role in crime prevention, working in partnership with other policing providers. What is important is that this approach appears to be a 'step up' in terms of how PCSOs are regarded by the police organisation as a whole. It appears that the national overseeing body (the College of Policing) for police training may be preparing PCSOs for an increased role in the policing family.

Further reading

Caless, B. (2007) '"Numties in yellow jackets": the nature of hostility towards the Police Community Support Officer in Neighbourhood Policing Teams', *Policing*, vol 1, no 2, pp 187-95.

Crawford, A. (2014) 'Police, policing and the future of the policing family', in J.M. Brown (ed) *The Future of Policing*, Abingdon: Routledge.

Crawford, A., Lister, S., Blackburn, S. and Burnett, J. (2005) *Plural Policing: The Mixed Economy of Visible Patrols in England and Wales*, Bristol: Policy Press.

Greig-Midlane, J. (2014) *Changing the beat? The impact of austerity on the neighbourhood policing workforce,* Cardiff: Cardiff University Press.

Innes, M. (2007) 'The reassurance function', *Policing*, vol 1, no 2, pp 132-41.

Jones, T. and Newburn, T. (2006) *Plural Policing: A Comparative Perspective*, Abingdon: Routledge

O'Neill, M. (2014a) 'Ripe for the chop or the public face of policing? PCSOs and neighbourhood policing in austerity', *Policing*, vol 8, no 3, pp 265-73.

PCSO (2014) PCSO website, available at www.gov.uk/police-community-support-officers-what-they-are (accessed 26 November 2015).

Storch, R. (1975) 'The plague of the blue locusts: police reform and popular resistance in Northern England, 1840–57, *International Revue of Social History*, Vol 20,

Terpstra, J., Van Stokkom, B. and Spreeuwers, R. (2013) *Who Patrols the Streets?*, The Hague: Eleven International Publishing.

SIX

The rise of
the volunteer

Introduction

This chapter considers the greater use of special constables and other volunteers within the pluralised policing framework, and reflects on the political will to introduce volunteers via the concept of the 'Big Society' and similar schemes. In addition, a discussion concerning the idea of the 'active or expert citizen' is considered. This concept, if successful, would necessitate a change in attitude from the police towards the use of volunteers.

Citizen participation in policing has long been understood as a response to wide-ranging grievances. The concept has evolved, however, and, as Bullock (2014) points out, has moved from focusing purely on re-establishing the principle of policing by consent and affirming the legitimacy of the police, to include more recent concerns around the wider themes of building capacity, generating social capital and reviving structures of democracy. In this respect, the legitimacy of the police may be assisted by the recruitment of volunteers with wide-ranging backgrounds and characteristics that better reflect those more recent of the community. Appeals to the citizen and the community as a whole are at the heart of current policing ideas, especially in the pluralised world of policing. However, 'community' itself is a contested and complex idea that is portrayed differently according to its need. For example, the general term 'community' is portrayed as a positive image, homogenous and consistent. 'Community' is used to describe many different ideas, including that of geographic location. However, 'community' may best be understood not as a local area where people live, but as a network of social relationships that people have and maintain, which ties people together. The introduction of social media and networking has challenged our idea of 'community' (Castells, 2010). People dip in and out of social networks more easily, and can be networked thus in many different ways. All of these ideas have an impact on our concept and understanding of the term 'community'. Despite this, appeals to the community for volunteers to support police activity is an important one for the new world of plural policing, and nowhere is this better evidenced than in the use of the special constabulary.

The special constabulary

The Police Act 1964 is generally considered to be the Act that established the modern special constabulary. Each force has its own special constabulary comprising volunteers who commit at least four hours per week to working with and supporting regular police officers. They wear similar uniforms and have the same powers as regular officers. 'Specials', as they are now commonly referred to, are also subject to the same rules of conduct and disciplinary procedures as sworn officers. In the past, specials have been subject to some abuse – being labelled as 'hobby-bobbies', for example (Berry et al, 1998); problems surrounding integration and communication between specials and the regular police have also occurred. However, they are representative of their community and have played a vital part in the neighbourhood policing approach. They are also an important component of that form of plural policing. However, the idea of special police is much older than the Police Act of 1964, and this historical context is worthy of examination in order to understand the reasons behind the importance of the volunteer police officer's role.

The historical context of special constables

The Anglo-Saxon period is identified by many (Lee, 1901; Critchley, 1978) as the context for the formal establishment of the idea of community involvement in crime control. The Norman Conquest adapted Anglo-Saxon arrangements into the Frankpledge system, which was communal, local and mutually beneficial for the community (Lee, 1901). However, the reasons behind this introduction of social control at a local and community level could be found at the highest echelons of Norman administration and society. Stead (1985) observes that this system was a distinct and workable model of social control. The model eventually evolved into a five-tier hierarchy of constables, each responsible for different aspects of governance and control. These included the 'tip' in the royal court, followed by the constable of the castle, the head constable of the shire, the high constable of the hundred and the petty constable of a tything or manor.

The Statute of Westminster in 1285 rationalised the system and confirmed the duty or obligation of everyone to maintain the peace, and if necessary arrest an offender. In addition, the unpaid part-time constable was to be supported in towns and cities by a 'watch' of up to 16 men on duty during the hours of darkness, who held the power to arrest strangers. The constable was responsible for maintaining the 'roster' of all those eligible and for allocating their duties.

The statute also stated that if an offender was not caught immediately, the ancient practice of 'hue and cry' could be employed; this obliged most people to keep certain weapons for this and other public services. Finally, the constable was required to present the offender at court.

Critchley (1978) states that the statute represented a fusion of Saxon and Norman influences; it reshaped the role of the part-time constable as one that carried a touch of regal authority, but was nonetheless still welded to the Anglo-Saxon principles of providing a personal service to the community and exercising common law powers of arrest. The seeds of the present-day special constable are thought to be found here.

With the introduction of the Justice of the Peace Act of 1361, justices were created to work alongside constables at a local level, but were of a higher social status, being permanent appointments and more formally linked to the crown. The annually appointed parish constables, who were now in charge or carrying out the policies of the justice, subsequently became responsible merely for law enforcement. Henceforth, the status of the parish constable gradually diminished, until by the mid-16th century it had become a burdensome and unattractive official position. Many who could avoid taking up the post by paying for a substitute did so. Interestingly, when examining the period from 1650 to 1900, Gill and Mawby (1990) utilise a phrase that has resonance for the modern pluralised policing environment. They suggest that during this period, a 'mixed economy' of policing emerged, during which the role of the publically paid police gradually gained ascendency, but never fully achieved monopoly status.

As society changed and ultimately became more industrialised, episodes of civil unrest and extensive rioting took place. Newly developing public police systems, while generally concerned with everyday crime, were also utilised to deal with major disturbances. The use of voluntary groups was common; these essentially formed a reserve force that could be mobilised at short notice to control specific, local incidents of public disorder. This voluntary aspect is perhaps the best context in which to view the origins of the modern special constabulary. In particular, section 15 of the Act for Better Relief of 1662 created a specific role for magistrates, whereby they could nominate local citizens to be sworn in for a year to be used in case of emergencies. However, there is little evidence or historical mention of its use until the 19th century when, at the beginning of the century, measures were introduced to promote the use of reserve forces. An Act of 1801 allowed for specials to be paid expenses, and in 1803, under threat of a French invasion, the government invoked magistrates to enlist individuals deemed to be trustworthy for the role. Specials were present at disturbances such as Peterloo (Manchester) in 1819, and in London (1820). In 1820, magistrates were allowed to appoint special constables not only in cases of public disorder, but also as a preventative measure when they anticipated trouble. The idea of a more permanent reserve force was clearly taking shape. The Special Constables Act of 1831 is generally credited with providing the basis of the special constabulary today, despite many amendments since introduced. During the 19th century, the use of specials to support and augment the regular police in the face of public disorder increased. Palmer (1990) highlights this by pointing to the fact that during the reform disorders of 1866, London Trades organised a force of 10,000 'keep the peace' special constables, while some 12,000 specials turned out for the 1867 reform demonstrations. During the Fenian Rising of 1876, a rebellion against British rule in Ireland, it is estimated that 115,000 voluntary specials served throughout England.

The special constabulary today

Generally speaking, a special's main role is to conduct local, intelligence-based patrols and to take part in crime prevention initiatives, often targeted at specific problem areas. In many forces, specials are also involved in policing major incidents, and in providing operational support to regular officers. Depending on which force they are attached to, specials generally engage in the following activities:

- conducting foot patrols;
- assisting at the scene of accidents, fights or fires;
- enforcing road safety initiatives;
- conducting house-to-house enquiries;
- providing security at major events;
- presenting evidence in court;
- tackling antisocial behaviour;
- tackling alcohol-related incidents;
- educating young people in local schools about crime reduction and community safety.

The number of specials has varied over time, with Bullock (2014) suggesting a peak of over 67,000 in the 1950s. However, Gill and Mawby (1990) suggest that this number had fallen to about 15,000 by 1980. Suggested reasons for this reduction in numbers could include the removal of those less active members. During the past decade, the number of specials gradually declined until, by the mid-2000s, it stood at around 11,000. The current number of specials in England and Wales can be seen in Table 6.1.

Table 6.1: Numbers of 'specials' by force in England and Wales, March 2015

	Total			Minority ethnic		
	Male	Female	Total	Male	Female	Total
Avon & Somerset	320	133	453	14	1	15
Bedfordshire	159	68	227	14	2	16
Cambridgeshire	193	84	277	7	2	9
Cheshire	264	126	390	9	3	12
Cleveland	59	34	93	0	1	1
Cumbria	84	35	119	2	1	3
Derbyshire	152	60	212	12	2	14
Devon & Cornwall	439	234	673	1	1	2
Dorset	155	72	227	1	1	2
Durham	74	36	110	0	0	0
Essex	269	97	366	11	4	15
Gloucestershire	85	30	115	3	0	3
Greater Manchester	508	195	703	64	17	81
Hampshire	332	124	456	6	5	11
Hertfordshire	234	69	303	19	3	22
Humberside	262	154	416	3	5	8
Kent	207	41	248	6	1	7
Lancashire	262	114	376	23	8	31
Leicestershire	184	70	254	25	5	30
Lincolnshire	147	82	229	0	1	1
London, City of	46	15	61	4	1	5
Merseyside	215	94	309	9	5	14
Metropolitan Police	2,496	1,163	3,659	807	309	1,116
Norfolk	183	74	257	2	1	3
Northamptonshire	296	116	412	6	5	11
Northumbria	191	57	248	2	0	2

	Total			Minority ethnic		
	Male	Female	Total	Male	Female	Total
North Yorkshire	116	68	184	3	0	3
Nottinghamshire	164	88	252	9	2	11
South Yorkshire	264	179	443	12	14	26
Staffordshire	231	87	318	10	2	12
Suffolk	159	75	234	5	0	5
Surrey	98	24	122	3	2	5
Sussex	271	122	393	7	4	11
Thames Valley	396	166	562	26	7	33
Warwickshire	180	77	257	14	6	20
West Mercia	207	92	299	4	4	8
West Midlands	289	85	374	58	19	77
West Yorkshire	521	303	824	51	27	78
Wiltshire	124	52	176	3	0	3
Dyfed-Powys	103	44	147	0	0	0
Gwent	81	43	124	1	1	2
North Wales	77	54	131	0	0	0
South Wales	55	13	68	55	13	68
Total all 43 forces	11,152	4,949	16,101	1,311	485	1,796
Total	11,349	4,982	16,331	1,335	485	1,820

Source: Home Office (2015)

According to these figures, the current strength of special constables stands at just over 16,000, with around 25 per cent of specials being female. In terms of ethnic diversity, 11 per cent of specials are minority ethnic officers, which is rather disappointing if one of the tenets of special constables is to increase diversity and thus assist in supporting the legitimation of the police among the wider community.

Clearly, under a new format of plural policing provision, possibly driven by austerity measures that involve fewer sworn officers but may include alternatives, the role of the special constable may become more important and numbers of such volunteers will need to increase if a uniformed presence is to be maintained within communities.

Why members of the public volunteer to become specials is, of course, open to debate, but one 'modern' suggestion revolves around the fact that, in the current economic climate, many forces are recruiting from within their 'policing family', which means preferential recruitment for special constables, PCSOs and other police staff. However, specials are only one example of volunteer support and citizen goodwill available to the police organisation.

The idea of citizen participation

Bullock (2014) suggests that the idea of civil society and civil participation has regained its importance in democratic theory and practice. Citizen participation is considered to be fundamental to the notion of civil society, as it is thought to help 'open up' those agencies involved within the governance of such a society. It has been postulated by some (for example, see Bullock, 2014) that allowing voluntary organisations to control functions currently being carried out by governments provides citizens with greater control over their affairs and the service they receive. The question remains, however, of whether citizens are really engaged enough with the process to be able to sustain such an approach. Nevertheless, the current political administration in England and Wales still appears to be wedded to the idea of greater civil participation in the delivery of public services, including in the delivery of policing. The idea of the 'Big Society', a flagship policy of the 2010 Conservative Party general election manifesto, and subsequently adopted by the Conservative–Liberal Democrat coalition government, involves the opening up of public services to a range of non-state providers, including community volunteers, and it still has momentum. Citizen participation via the role of the volunteer, therefore, is considered to be an important facet in the world of plural policing.

Big Society

In essence, the Big Society refers to a tripartite partnership between the citizen, the community and local government (Eaton, 2010). This vision requires families, networks and neighbourhoods in a postmodern society to formalise a working partnership that is effective and sustainable in its approach to solving problems, building social cohesion and setting priorities for Britain (BBC, 2010). In doing so, the government, along with the involvement of communities, aims to create a Big Society that is bigger, stronger and accountable to all. How this idea equates to the practicalities of living in the UK is worthy of examination. The current Prime Minister, David Cameron, a strong advocate of the Big Society, defines its ideology as one of liberalism, empowerment, freedom and responsibility, where the 'top-down' approach to government is abandoned and replaced by local innovation and civic action. Interestingly, critics of the government, including the general secretary of Unison, refer to the Big Society as the 'Big Cop-out', and brand it a scheme that is primarily concerned with cutting investment and saving money (ITN, 2010). This *laissez-faire* approach to government could spell the end for new public management and centralised performance indicators, as it will be the responsibility of British society and its communities to assess performance. However, the government insists that in order to work, the Big Society will require significant involvement, encouragement and support from communities. Prior to austerity measures and the change in government in 2010, five approaches or strands were considered fundamental to the idea of Big Society (Cabinet Office, 2010).

Empowering communities

The Big Society approach requires local people to have a greater say in the 'construction' of their surroundings. Accompanying these new powers, local people would have the means to save local facilities and services threatened by closure, if they were deemed to be fundamental to the fabric of society. Communities would also have the right to take over state-run services and facilities. Bringing about this change, the coalition government stated that it would recruit and train 'community organisers' to support the creation of neighbourhood ground all over the UK.

Action-orientated communities

Community involvement, philanthropy and a spirit of volunteerism are an integral component of the Big Society. The introduction of a Big Society day and a focus on civic service aimed to increase and stimulate involvement from community members of all socioeconomic backgrounds. A National Citizen Service was to be established to encourage young people to develop the skills needed in a modern society, to break down negative perceptions and stimulate cohesion.

Decentralised power

A drive for decentralisation and 'rolling back the frontiers of the state' are all perhaps synonymous with the style of governance exhibited by the Conservative Party in previous administrations. Reducing the size and influence of the state by stimulating local initiatives is perceived as a key driving force in the move to establish a Big Society. Greater autonomy, both financially and procedurally, was believed to be the way forward as the government moved away from micro-management or 'nano-level' management towards a 'macro-management' approach. This cultural change in governance would provide local authorities and local officials with greater discretion and influence over the direction of local policy. Decisions on housing and planning were also likely to return to local councils in an effort to make the procedure of allocation and urban design more accountable to local people.

More social enterprises

As pluralisation was to be encouraged, it was envisaged that there would be an expansion in the number of social enterprises. Those sectors, companies, industries and organisations that had previously been operating under a monopoly or oligopoly were likely to see an increase in competition as state-run functions were likely to be shared with other social enterprises such as collectives and charities. Public sector workers would be encouraged to set up employee-owned cooperatives, encouraging innovation and quality of service for the end user while being a more economically viable option for the state. Funding the Big Society was to come from dormant bank accounts, which, it was believed, would provide the necessary funding for stimulating neighbourhood groups, charities and social enterprise. However, as previously indicated, it was unlikely that the Big Society ideology drive would be funded by an unlimited supply of capital, and financial constraints would come to play a large part in the introduction and use of social enterprise.

Information ability

Finally, confidence in official data and statistics had been eroded in recent years with the publication of potentially unfounded, incorrect statistics resulting in several official apologies being made in parliament by senior ministers. Underpinning the Big Society, the government aimed to create a new culture whereby the public had a 'right to data' that would be published regularly in an attempt to improve accountability.

However, despite its promises, there appears to have been a hiatus in the delivery of the Big Society. There is currently very little discussion surrounding this idea, and the reason why it appears not to have caught hold and been as effective as it should have been are complex. However, for one critic, the answer is quite simple: not enough of the

Prime Minister's supporters actually believed in the idea, and austerity measures have meant that many of its important strands cannot be supported financially (Butler, 2015).

A different approach

It is useful to consider the concept of the Big Society against the backdrop of previous governments' activities within the field of crime and disorder reduction. The 'new' philosophy of the Big Society, it was argued, could be seen as an extension of previous governments' attempts to relocate responsibility for crime control from purely state-owned mechanisms to the ownership of communities. Garland (2001) argues that this country has seen the development of one type of community-style programme after another since the 1960s, with the result that 'the community' has become the all-purpose solution to every criminal justice problem. Some of these programmes have been viewed as being innovative and radical, seeking to respond to the concerns of citizens and enlist the help of neighbourhood residents and organisations. This ongoing attempt to extend the use of private sector and community agencies is described by Garland as a responsibilisation strategy, and involves a change in the manner in which governments respond to crime and disorder. Instead of addressing crime and disorder in a direct fashion by means of police and the criminal justice sanction approach, the new approach requires a new kind of indirect action.

Over the past decade or so, a new kind of crime prevention approach has been developed by Western governments, especially the UK, which has seen the introduction of new strategies dependent on such concepts as partnerships, alliances, inter-agency cooperation, the multi-agency approach, and activating citizens to name but a few (Rogers, 2012). The primary objective for this, however, has been to manoeuvre responsibility for crime control on to other agencies, organisations and individuals that operate outside the criminal justice system, and to persuade them to act appropriately in the management and prevention of crime (Hughes, 2007). However, in terms of the debate concerning community engagement, there is a need for partnership agencies to review their approach to consultation and engagement, to ensure that an informed public (as a result of better local information being available to them) are seen to be involved in the decision-making process concerning service delivery. This is in contrast to communities being loosely involved in operational decisions concerning the provision of services (Rogers and Milliner, 2010).

The use and encouragement of volunteers in the police service is one of historical significance. The role of the special constabulary in assisting with control public disorder, as well as latterly enhancing neighbourhood policing, is now well established. Citizen participation in such schemes as the local neighbourhood watch has arguably been supported by the police organisation, but not with as much vigour as it might have been. The same is true regarding the use of other volunteer schemes and community participation in the delivery of such services. While the utilisation of volunteers and citizen participation may not provide a panacea for the problems facing the delivery of policing, it can, in many respects, help to maintain local accountability and representativeness in policing as a whole. Volunteers are largely seen as a force for good by supporting police activity, acting as an alternative or supplemental source of security provision, promoting civil society and contributing to policing in a meaningful way (Bullock, 2014), One aim of volunteers is to influence the 'culture' of the police through increasing diversity and promoting greater understanding, but this influence is not yet evident. This may be one reason why levels of volunteering in the police service are generally low, although there are doubtless other factors. In the changing world of plural policing, however, a much greater reliance on the use of volunteers in their various formats is apparent. Issues surrounding ethical and professional behaviour, the acceptance of voluntary staff by the police culture and supporting volunteer accountability for their work are all issues that need to be carefully considered in a police world, which needs to support the rise of the volunteer (Bullock, 2014). In other aspects of policing, the police appear to have been reluctant to fully embrace the approach. However, the new and developing landscape of plural policing demands an increase in public involvement. Without this important aspect of future policing arrangements, police services to the public may be reduced, or could be taken up by private suppliers of security.

As with most public bodies, there is always potential within the police to improve the delivery of service to the community. Clearly, there is a need to further involve the community, promoting ownership and inter-cooperation in the delivery of policing. While accepting that volunteer schemes are not a panacea to all of these problems, they present a real and robust economic option that must be carefully considered. In addition to any economic advantage, improved community cohesion, increased public confidence and organisational transparency may be enhanced. As the economic downturn continues, meeting government targets will become increasingly difficult for the police and their partners. It will be the role of police managers, planners and their partners to ensure that front-line services remain efficient and public demands are met in an ever-challenging economic and social landscape; the use of volunteers, it is suggested, may be one way of helping to achieve this goal.

The role of the public in pluralised policing

Greater citizen intervention and participation is one possible route to reducing the harm and the financial cost of crime. Yet research shows only 30 per cent of Britons would feel confident about intervening to stop a group of 14-year-olds committing vandalism, in contrast to 60 per cent of Germans (ADT, 2006). Often citizens are worried that, if they do intervene, they might be attacked by the perpetrators, be arrested themselves by the police or be sued (Casey, 2008). The last of these is addressed by the Social Action, Responsibility and Heroism Bill (2014). This states that if something goes wrong when a person acts for the benefit of society (such as intervening in an emergency) and they are sued, the court will take full account of the context of their actions. However, the Bill does not address other risks, particularly the concern that promoting public action of this kind could increase the risk of vigilantism. Notwithstanding these concerns, public participation also comes with its own set of challenges. Citizens are rarely trained in the kind of negotiation and safety skills police constables require to deal with volatile incidents. However, an interesting initiative, the Woolwich model (Rogers and Milliner, 2010), puts forward the idea of training citizens to deal with antisocial behaviour in their local community in much the same way as first-aiders are trained to respond to health emergencies.

Encouraging citizens to volunteer can also be a challenge. The Citizen Power Project to encourage public participation created stronger connections between people and develop new models of citizen-led response. Although the project has had some success in galvanising residents, participants tended to be either 'superhuman altruists' or 'busybodies', that is individuals who are very good at managing their time and becoming involved in community work, or those individuals who are just keen to know other people's problems. A large number were only willing to engage when the right opportunities, incentives and support were in place (O'Brien, 2011). Research shows that graduates and affluent residents are more likely to volunteer to attend police meetings, join neighbourhood watch schemes and engage in other activities of this kind (Bullock and Sindall, 2014), which raises the issue of how to avoid simply recruiting 'the usual suspects' and motivate the 'harder-to-reach' groups. Fragmented, transient communities are often those most distanced from policing (Curtis and James, 2013), and the most vulnerable to crime. The confidence to intervene to prevent disorder, or to approach the police and report wrongdoing, is often dependent on how much these communities trust the police to support them. Finally, citizens may not know the best way to negotiate with a perpetrator to achieve a peaceful outcome. They may believe they are standing up for a common morality or higher purpose, but may use violent means to make their point. Without the accountability of a corporate or service structure, they may also make mistakes, such as in the case in 2000 of a doctor hounded from her home when citizens misunderstood the meaning of the word 'paediatrician', thinking it meant 'paedophile' (Allison, 2000). In times of austerity, then, one of the major drivers for encouraging and supporting the drive for volunteers must surely be the area of cost and budget reduction.

The cost of volunteer policing

Policing Britain costs billions of pounds every year. In a report published by the Chancellor of the Exchequer, following the comprehensive spending review in 2007, the Home Office budget was set to exceed £10 billion pounds by 2010, perhaps demonstrating the enormity of the costs involved with policing (HM Treasury, 2007). It is certainly a challenge to ensure maximum efficiency, effectiveness and economic value for every pound spent. The Taxpayers' Alliance estimates that the total cost of recorded crime alone, incorporating both economic and social impact, stands at £15 billion per annum, calculated to cost on average almost £275 per person (Sinclair and Taylor, 2008). The calculated economic cost differed between forces; the highest recorded cost rose to £389.94, with the lowest costing only £130.26. Table 6.2 illustrates these differences.

Policing has always been a complex issue, with the police and their partners having to deal with the results of social changes, the forces of globalisation and advances in technology, both today and throughout history. They must constantly adapt to reflect such changes, finding new ways to ensure that forces provide an effective, efficient and appropriate service (Gravelle and Rogers, 2009; 2010).

Table 6.2: The cost of crime per person by police area

Police force	Total cost of crime	Population	Cost of crime per person
Nottinghamshire Police	£411,579,162	1,055,500	£389.94
Metropolitan Police	£2,913,533,525	7,512,400	£387.83
Humberside Police	£343,465,441	905,000	£379.52
Greater Manchester Police	£951,801,569	2,553,700	£372.71
Norfolk Constabulary	£165,764,291	832,400	£199.14
Surrey Police	£210,857,216	1,085,200	£194.30
Dyfed Powys Police	£93,573,002	503,600	£185.81
North Yorkshire Police	£102,043,558	783,400	£130.26

Source: Cited in Sinclair and Taylor (2008, p 12).

Neighbourhood volunteers

Neighbourhood volunteers are members of the public who have expressed an interest in working with the police, undertaking various roles and responsibilities within the organisation. However, they are not special constables and so possess no police powers or warrants. These neighbourhood volunteers assist when they can; many volunteers enjoy this flexibility when supporting the service and their local community. Depending on whether their role is administrative or involves some sort of community engagement, some volunteers work from different police stations while others work on the street engaging with members of the public directly. These volunteers may also engage in Policing and Communities Together (PACT) meetings, letter dropping and other operations, often working alongside neighbourhood police teams and partner agencies. One of the major utilisers of volunteers is Lancashire Constabulary. Currently, Lancashire has 644 volunteers, from varied backgrounds and age groups. Of this total, 55 volunteers are aged over 70 and represent various elements from within society (Flanagan, 2008b). To ensure that volunteers are representative of the community and fully reflect its demographic make-up, most police services will attempt to recruit individuals of different backgrounds, ages, ethnic minorities and religions. In many cases across the country, this could include university or college students, those retired and others from diverse communities. Having applied, volunteers are usually 'vetted' and receive training to better equip them for working within the police organisation. In order to assist with their work, some forces have opted to dedicate specialist police officers to deal with neighbourhood volunteer schemes, whereas others have designed a new administrative position, often referred to as a volunteer coordinator. The role of the coordinator is to oversee the recruitment and welfare of volunteers and to generally manage all operations, issues, concerns, training, recruitment, advertising and financial expenditure relating to volunteers. Involving the public in different volunteer schemes has many advantages, not least the additional human resources gained. This is especially useful when faced with the prospect of a diminishing supply of funding and an increasing demand for service delivery. Inclusion and engagement with the community will not only make the delivery of policing more transparent, but will, given time, create a sense of ownership and pride among the community itself, resulting in an improved relationship between the public and the police service. Volunteer schemes may have a positive influence because of the extended partnership approach, and improved confidence and cooperation. The improved relationship, as well as the increased sense of ownership and inclusion, may well result in targets for community safety being met. This may arise in part from greater public engagement with local voluntary initiatives, such as PACT meetings and neighbourhood watch. As a direct consequence, this may lead to a decrease in overall crime levels as well as and fear of crime, which could lead in turn to leading to a reduction in the reassurance gap. Fear of crime, whether rational or irrational, is a matter of perception, and for the public perception is reality. As actual crime reduces, so too does the fear of crime; if the reduction in real crime rates is combined with the public's perception that crime is reducing, this results in a reduction in the reassurance gap (McLaughlin and Muncie, 2006). Indeed, the overall product of effective community engagement should not be underestimated. A report by Her Majesty's Inspectorate of Constabulary noted that the role of the volunteer was vital in the fight against crime (Flanagan, 2008a). The report concludes that the work being carried out by the volunteers, which includes PACT coordination, reassurance call-backs and other initiatives, is having a positive impact. Subsequently, there has been an improvement in the service provided by the public, a more diverse representation of the community within the constabulary and an overall increase in public confidence shown towards the police.

In addition to perceived improved community cohesion, increased public confidence and greater transparency, volunteer schemes have a clear economic advantage. In times of economic downturn, as previously noted, economic advantages need to be considered seriously. When assessing the economic impact of any volunteer scheme, many organisations use the volunteer investment value audit or VIVA (IVR, 2003). Effective evaluations need to incorporate many different factors when assessing impact, including the effect the scheme may have on the organisation, volunteers and the wider community. In addition, evaluations should include a comprehensive capital investment appraisal, comprising economic, physical, social, human and cultural aspects (IVR, 2003). Published by the Institute for Volunteering (IVR, 2003), the VIVA has become an important framework when assessing economic impact on organisations. In essence, the audit is a measuring tool, designed to calculate outputs that include the value of volunteer time, or total salary savings against inputs that may constitute staff salaries or training costs.

A good example of the financial impact volunteers can have is illustrated in a scheme run by Lancashire Police in 2008. At this time, Lancashire Police had 644 volunteers (Flanagan, 2008b). Table 6.3 demonstrates how economic advantages are calculated in terms of volunteer value, using the example of the Lancashire Police community volunteer scheme. The first column demonstrates the variety of roles being performed by each of the volunteers, including administration, support and public duties. For the purposes of this example, the lowest possible pay scale has been used, assessed at just over £6.29 per hour. As published in a Home Office (2007) report, the volunteers delivered a combined total of 3,626 hours per month, or 906.5 hours per week. This weekly total is then multiplied by the number of weeks in a year, excluding public holidays, which provides the total number of volunteer hours delivered in one year. By using the lowest possible pay grade, the yearly volunteer hours multiplied by this pay grade suggests that the total saving in terms of staff wages for the force is £273,690.48. Having calculated the total volunteer value, or total wages being saved, it is necessary to include employment overheads. This will take into account costs for the organisation, including national insurance, holiday pay and other expenses. For this, a total of 20 per cent is added to the volunteer value, bringing the total saving to approximately £328,429.44 a year.

The VIVA approach has been found to be beneficial for organisations by enabling them to develop more effective management information on the use of volunteers; as a result, it aids strategic planning and results in improved cost-effectiveness. Used widely by many charities and well-known organisations since its creation in 1996, this is a method approved by both the National Centre for Volunteering and the UK government.

Table 6.3: The economic impact on the Lancashire Police of its volunteer schemes

Volunteer or role title	Equivalent paid job	Hourly wage rate for job	Total weekly hours in this role (All)	x 48 or number of weeks per year worked by volunteers	x hourly wage rate = value of this role in a year
PACT coordinator/ reassurance call-back, front desk, etc	Lowest pay scale for police staff	£6.2914 (calculated from current administrative staff salary)	906.5	906.5 x 48 = 43,512	30,912 x £6.2914 = £273,690.48

The Lancashire example

The introduction of a neighbourhood volunteer scheme in Lancashire is worthy of further examination. Here, the police service is currently recruiting volunteers from the local community, aiming to improve relations between the force and the locality it serves. Launched in June 2004, there are currently 644 volunteers, encompassing different ages, ethnic groups, genders and backgrounds (Flanagan, 2008b). Consequently, Lancashire now has some 55 volunteers over the age of 70, a group that the police service in general has difficulty engaging with. Clearly, by encouraging cooperation with these groups, new relationships can be formed. Volunteers perform different roles, including neighbourhood policing, quality of service auditing, administrative duties and dealing with public enquiries. A volunteer scheme of this size will inevitably have major implications for the service. For example, having extra staff means extra physical resources, which reduces pressure on front-line services and allows police officers to return to front-line duties; this helps to meet a key objective for many chief police officers, which is to increase high-visibility policing. To employ this number of part-time staff would be economically prohibitive, and almost impossible for police forces to sustain. Indeed, using volunteers could potentially save hundreds of thousands of pounds a year for the police service; for each hour a volunteer works, there is a saving for the police and over one year the savings are considerable, as demonstrated by Lancashire Police, which saved £328,429.44 per annum through its volunteer scheme. In addition to the economic advantages attached to the use of volunteers with the police organisation itself, there is an increased need for people within communities to participate more in local crime and disorder control.

Lancashire Police are still actively engaging volunteers in their citizen volunteer schemes, with volunteers performing administrative duties and operating CCTV cameras among other activities (see www. lancashire.police.uk/join-us/volunteers.aspx).

The expert citizen

Despite the budgetary reductions implemented thus far, and the associated government confidence in the impact of these reductions on policing (Fraser et al, 2014), the Institute of Fiscal Studies (IFS) (2015) predicts that public agency budget reductions in the UK still have a long way to go. Indeed, if the IFS report is to be believed, the worst spending cuts have yet to be seen. The impact of these reductions will see the introduction of a 'new' police in England and Wales, one that is drastically reduced in numbers and focuses on core functions involving crime detection at the expense of community engagement. This 'new' police will be locally accountable to the Police and Crime Commissioner or equivalent body, and will herald a new form of plural policing for local communities. Should this be the case, the way in which the police will continue to function in a democratically accountable policing model with such reduced resources is a question worthy of deeper examination. In particular, it is worth enquiring how the public face of that model, which in England and Wales manifests itself in the idea of community policing and its visible representation in the form of neighbourhood policing teams, will satisfy the fundamentals of this approach. One suggestion is to encourage greater involvement of the community in policing through the concept of the 'expert citizen'.

Who are expert citizens?

This type of community approach requires the police to adopt a new way of working in order to maximise available resources, so that they may be able to cope with the financial and other pressures likely to impinge on them. A key element of this is the concept of the expert citizen. Popularised by the Danish political theorist Henrik Bang (2005), the expert citizen idea suggests individuals (living within and from the community) who are equipped with the relevant knowledge, understanding and skills to enable them to actively participate in efforts to improve community life. Bang distinguishes between the expert citizen and the 'everyday maker' in his work. Both categories of political identity describe the activities of informed and empowered individuals within political life, though some differences are suggested in terms of their affiliations, levels of participation and self-interest.

For Fraser and colleagues (2014, p 18), the expert citizen:

> [...] would be one who not only reduces demand on the police service through taking steps to keep their person and property safe, but also through all of their interactions with the police service.

Thus the expert citizen in a policing context is someone who not only knows about locks, bolts and other situational crime prevention techniques, but also possesses knowledge of the requirements of police systems (such as the 999 and 101 telephone systems in the UK). They may also volunteer information, act as witnesses and proactively engage with the police. The expert citizen would undoubtedly be encouraged and supported to develop a range of 'community skills' (analogous to first aid in the workplace). Participation would, it is assumed, follow different routes and levels of intensity, from *ad hoc* engagements on specific problems to more routine participation as part of a police or community volunteer scheme.

Challenges for the expert citizen

While suggesting distinct possibilities for improved police–public relations and positive developments in policing and community life, the expert citizen concept also raises certain counter-issues that are worthy of attention, some of which are summarised below:

- The concept may be seen as imprecise and vacuous: for example, what does it mean? How does the citizen become 'expert'? How is the idea of expert defined? Who decides on and confers expert status?
- Following Bang (2005), how would issues of self-interest and/or ideology be addressed in the selection of and engagement with expert citizens?
- How would police organisations (and communities) ensure that there is expert citizen representation from among a diverse range of community groups?
- Is the intention to create a society of expert citizens, or is the plan more limited in its focus, and aimed only at specific and targeted individuals?

- Is there a suggested or required level of participation required for the citizen expert?
- There may be police resistance to the idea (police culture is notoriously resistant to change and has a propensity towards suspicion of 'non-police' input).
- There may be public resistance, whereby individuals and groups reject calls to become expert citizens either because they do not want to accept the responsibility, or through fear of reprisals and so on).

The expert citizen as a community bridge

The expert citizen approach acknowledges that a major feature of improving policing, and equipping it to cope with a range of pressures in the future, is to encourage the police to develop a better understanding of demand. This goes beyond merely monitoring the calls for assistance that come to the police organisation; rather, it extends the idea of 'understanding demand' to include improved identification of local community needs and expectations. It also encompasses an improved internal understanding of the police organisation's own cultural dispositions as well as its skills base, in addition to an enhanced understanding of the priorities and capabilities of partner agencies. Expert citizens clearly have a major role to play in this context as they have the potential to act as an asset, able and prepared to speak on behalf of local people in ways that account for local experiences as well as possessing an understanding of police organisational requirements.

Of course, the concept of the citizen is already familiar within policing discourses: the 'active citizen' and 'citizen-focused policing' are two relatively well-established terms (for example, see Lloyd and Foster, 2009). The notion of the expert citizen implies something different and arguably more sophisticated: while the expert citizen is likely to be an active and participating citizen, the emphasis and requirement will be that such involvement will be undertaken in an informed, knowledgeable, reflective and purposeful way.

Conclusion

Clearly, the future provision of policing services in England and Wales, as in many other countries, is likely to alter drastically. Budgetary constraints, the ongoing police reform project and the continued focus on perceived core values such as fighting crime and dealing with global criminality such as terrorist activities may mean a reduction in resources for more community-focused, engagement-style policing practices.

In turn, this may lead to a 'disconnect' between communities and the police, which actually works against core policing values and activities. One way of maintaining close contact with the community, while ensuring crime prevention and interaction remain viable, is perhaps to encourage citizens to actively participate in 'self-policing' through volunteer work with the police. This is manifested in the ideas of the special constabulary and the activities of groups such as neighbourhood watch and neighbourhood volunteers, as well as the newer idea of the expert citizen. The identification, development of and collaboration with such individuals and groups can be seen as representing a more tailored, measured and economical approach by the police, one that opens up a new set of possibilities for police–community connection within a plural policing model that continues to value its democratic associations. Despite any drawbacks associated with such ideas, it seems increasingly likely that police forces in England and Wales will need to carefully consider the advantages of such an approach, to assist in maintaining the link between the police and the community that is vital for the democratic policing model to survive.

Further reading

Bang, H. (2005) 'Among everyday makers and expert citizens', in J. Newman (ed) *Remaking Governance*, Bristol: Policy Press, pp 159-79.

Bullock, K. (2014) 'Introduction', in *Citizens, Community and Crime Control*, Palgrave Macmillan UK, pp 1-24.

Bullock, K. and Sindall, K. (2014) 'Examining the nature and extent of public participation in neighbourhood policing', *Policing and Society*, vol 24, no 4, pp 385-404.

Eaton, G. (2010) *The 'Big Society': New Doubts Emerge*, London: New Statesman.

Fraser, C., Hagelund, C., Sawyer, K. and Stacey, M. (2014) 'The expert citizen, reform ideas', available at www.reform.uk/publication/the-expert-citizen

Gill, M.L. and Mawby, R.I. (1990) *A Special Constable: A Study of the Police Reserve*, Aldershot: Averbury.

Gravelle, J. and Rogers, C. (2009) 'Your country needs you: the economic viability of volunteers in the police', *Safer Communities: A Journal of Practice, Opinion, Policy and Research*, vol 8, no 3, pp 12-14.

Gravelle, J. and Rogers, C. (2010) 'The Economy of Policing: The Impact of the Volunteer', *Policing: A Journal of Policy and Practice*, 4 (1), 56-63.

Halpern, D. (2007) *Social Capital*, Cambridge: Polity Press.

Kretzmann, J.P. and McKnight, J.L. (1993) *Building Communities from the Inside Out: A Path toward Finding and Mobilizing a Community's Assets*, Evanston, IL: Institute for Policy Research.

SEVEN

Partnerships or plural policing?

Introduction

Pluralised policing is, of course, a phrase that encourages the partnership approach to providing services to the public. Neighbourhood policing teams are, in a sense, an historical example of the partnership approach in terms of the delivery of policing at the local level. The partnership approach, therefore, is an important facet of the idea of pluralised policing and worthy of examination. In recent years, the notion of community safety partnerships – which focus primarily on crime prevention – and the idea of public–private partnerships (PPPs) with private security companies such as G4S have both come to the fore. This chapter focuses on these two major ideas, which illustrate that agencies other than the police organisation have been involved in policing for some time.

Since the introduction of the Crime and Disorder Act 1998, the police organisation has been legally obliged to engage in partnership work with many other agencies involved in crime prevention activities. These agencies began to 'police' their geographic areas alongside the public police and are, in effect, engaged in plural-style policing.

Historical context of community safety partnerships

It is difficult to identify precisely when the concept of partnerships first entered the debate on policing and crime prevention. 'Partnership' in this sense refers to a purposeful relationship between the police and the public, or between the police and other agencies in this field. The debate on policing does not appear to have mentioned the concept until the rise of community policing in the early 1980s; since then, the idea that the police could no longer tackle crime alone has developed into something more than a slogan. It was during this time that the Home Office promoted a number of initiatives, including the formation of the Home Office Crime Prevention Unit, while various Home Office circulars, including Circular 8/1984 (Home Office, 1984), encouraged all agencies to become involved in crime prevention. The then Conservative government supported the launch of Crime Concern in 1988 and thereafter supervised the development of the Safer Cities initiative, which has been the catalyst for many later crime prevention partnerships in this country. The success of the Safer Cities initiative may be attributed to the need for economic and social regeneration and the propensity for social unrest in these centres. A common factor in these schemes was the involvement of the police, local government and other bodies in a form of partnerships; as a result, it was argued that this was a sound approach for effective community safety and crime prevention work. Perhaps one of the most influential documents to be published during this period was the report of the Standing Committee on Crime Prevention, chaired by James Morgan, which was responsible for reviewing the development of crime prevention. This report, later known as the Morgan report (Home Office, 1991), contained many proposals for the structure and coordination of crime prevention strategies, and in particular highlighted the need for the partnership approach with an increased emphasis on the role of local authorities. It may be argued, then, that the rise in popularity of the partnership approach for controlling crime and disorder was relatively dramatic; as such, an historical analysis of the origins of this particular approach is necessary for further understanding. Additionally, a clear analysis of the component parts of the partnership approach is required. These component parts usually comprise a style of policing that is considered unusual, or different in some way from the normal reactive style of policing, in addition to various crime prevention techniques. These techniques appear to contain elements of situational crime prevention and include a consideration of repeat victims of specific crimes. Partnerships also purport to include wide consultation with the community they serve, an important component element discussed elsewhere in this book.

The past 30 years have produced a substantial amount of research into partnership working and advisory pieces for the police service, urging it to tackle problems with the aid of the community and other agencies. Many of the publications encouraging this approach stem from the Home Office; a typical example of the mood for change can be seen in the influential Home Office Circular 8/1984, which states:

> Every individual citizen and all those agencies whose policies and practices can influence the extent of crime should make their contribution. Preventing crime is a task for the whole community. (Home Office, 1984, p 1)

Thus, the drive for partnership working was intended to be centrally driven but locally delivered, and was to be fundamentally evidence-based in its approach.

Kirkholt and other initiatives

The message could not have been clearer for police services. Consequently, throughout the country partnership initiatives were introduced. Initiatives such as the Kirkholt Burglary Prevention Project (Forrester et al, 1988; 1990) were promoted as flagships of the partnership approach, and the police service was encouraged to engage with other agencies in community crime prevention initiatives. For a number of years, the Home Office sponsored and published research into specific areas of tackling criminality that appeared to highlight the successful approach of partnerships involving different agencies. These initiatives covered a range of offences from burglary (Brown, 1997) to public order and annoyance on housing estates (Morris, 1996) and thefts against retail outlets (Tilley, 1993). The common claim of all this research was that positive results were obtained by several agencies collaborating to tackle highly specific crimes. Indeed, such was the faith in the partnership approach that the Home Office published a document containing examples of partnership initiatives from various locations around the UK that were considered good practice (Home Office, 1997). The intention of this document, it was claimed, was to provide a framework of ideas for those agencies not already engaged in the paradigm of partnership policing.

One of the main reasons behind the introduction of the partnership approach lay in the fact that there had been a rise in recorded crime, coupled with the realisation that the police did not have the resources to tackle this problem alone.

The Morgan report

The Crime Prevention Circular 8/1984 (Home Office, 1984) was seen as a watershed in crime prevention policy. Its emphasis lay in the principle that crime prevention must be accepted as a significant and integral goal of public policy, both centrally and locally. In this circular, particular importance was placed on the need for a coordinated approach to crime prevention and joint strategies involving partnerships against crime. Although more often rhetoric than reality, the idea of multi-agency 'partnerships' took hold around the country. A pluralised approach to crime prevention had clearly arrived in Britain.

Effectively, the guiding idea of community safety was heralded as a way of moving beyond a situational definition of crime prevention (which focused on the management, design and manipulation of the built physical environment) to a broader social definition (which sought to change the perceived criminal motivations within people by affecting the social environment).

By the end of the 1980s, the Home Office circular *Tackling Crime* (Home Office, 1989) showed the further development of the partnership between police and community, increasing their commitment to crime prevention. Particular attention was paid to the problem of coordination, or rather the lack of it, between the agencies that make up the criminal justice system. This circular paved the way for what was widely considered to be the key inspiration for many subsequent crime prevention schemes adopted by local governments and other social and multi-agency bodies during the 1990s: the Morgan report (Home Office, 1991).

The report went on to identify six key elements in need of attention: structure, leadership, information, identity, durability and resources. These areas, the report argued, needed to be addressed in order to improve the organisation and delivery of multi-agency crime prevention. The report also supported the notion that local authorities be given the statutory duty (and therefore the resources) to coordinate crime prevention/community safety strategies for their locality. The report went on to argue that sufficient resources to make this change must be forthcoming from central government. (In passing, it may be noted that the recommendations regarding both local authorities' statutory role and resourcing were not taken up by the government during the 1990s, probably due to its concerns over costs and its ideological hostility to local government per se.) With the enactment of the Crime and Disorder Act 1998 (Home Office, 1998), a statutory partnership was introduced, instead of Morgan's recommendation of a leadership role for local authorities. Further, the Labour Party's proposals as part of this Act stated that no extra resources would be given to local authorities to meet their new statutory responsibilities for crime prevention. Despite the limitations this placed on local authorities at the time, however, it must be recognised that much of the Morgan report's philosophy of partnerships, multi-agency collaboration, and audits are at the forefront of current crime prevention policy proposals (Home Office, 1997; 2005).

Hughes (1998) views the Morgan report as a report written by local authority and police officers for executive officers. In particular, the question of how these multi-agency partnership officer groups relate to issues of democratic accountability, he argues, is never fully addressed. Further, Hughes suggests that citizens are being called on to play a crucial role in crime prevention through their own actions. As in other social policy areas, there is an appeal to the much-vaunted but ill-defined 'active citizen' to play a key role, in this case in both crime surveillance and 'policing'. The Home Office pamphlet *Partners against Crime* (Home Office, 1994) confidently asserted that the power of partnerships in beating crime was proved and three complementary partnerships were presented as initiatives to be launched or given further encouragement nationally in 1995. These were the already well-established neighbourhood watch schemes, street watch and the introduction of neighbourhood constables.

The idea of community safety

The publication of the Morgan report (Home Office, 1991) also saw the term 'crime prevention' replaced by the concept of 'community safety' in order to broaden the base of support for such partnerships. The term 'crime prevention' is often narrowly interpreted, and this reinforces the view that it is solely the responsibility of the police. On the other hand, the term 'community safety' is open to wider interpretation and has the potential to encourage greater participation from all sections of the community (Home Office, 1991).

Since the review of the Crime and Disorder Act 2006, crime and disorder reduction partnerships are now commonly referred to as community safety partnerships in both England and Wales. By employing the term 'community', it was hoped that this approach would be more acceptable to the public at large for, as Cohen (1985) rightly points out, the word 'community' appeals to an individual's perceptions of positive feelings. When the imagery portrayed is positive, the term is associated with other positive adjectives, such as 'natural' or 'integrative', or with positive concepts such as 'openness'. Therefore, institutions such as community centres, community prisons and community policing are generally viewed as positive and non-threatening.

Central to the idea of partnerships is the need for a wide consultation process that involves the relevant public agencies, private businesses and the community. For partnerships trying to provide this service, the aims of this consultation process can be listed as follows:

• To reach as broad a cross-section of the population as possible. All parties, it is argued, have an interest in consulting as widely and deeply as possible, as failure to do so could mean that prominent crime and disorder problems are not brought to their attention.

- To identify public priorities to influence the annual policing plan, which ultimately helps target valuable police resources to particular community concerns.
- To identify public priorities for local action, so that local partnerships can be focused on individual community problems such as the perception of youth annoyance.
- To provide the public with information on policing and community safety matters, feeding back information to the public and improving the quality of consultation.

Response to partnerships

Partnerships are concerned with the management of a service provided to the community and, therefore, organisational attainments are quite high on their list of consultation priorities. For the public, according to Elliot and Nicholls (1996), the main reason for engaging in the consultation process with policing partnerships seems to revolve around two main areas of concern, namely:

- obtaining rapid police action on public concerns; this means it is likely that the public do not merely wish to be consulted on their views, as their priority is to get the police to address their problems;
- obtaining information from the police, such as what the police are doing, how they are performing, and the impact they are having on crime. They may well see consultation as a way to achieve this.

However, the consultation process itself, albeit a positive idea, is far from infallible. Public meetings, where the community is asked to attend to air its views, are not necessarily representative of the community as a whole. Marginalised groups such as gay and lesbian groups, young people and those regarded as outsiders because of their minority ethnic background, are often not represented at such consultation processes. Consequently, the concerns addressed are those that are normally voiced, it could be argued, by locally elected representatives and other community leaders who may not be acting on behalf of the whole community.

Asset-based community development

Another interesting and arguably underdeveloped theme within the community safety partnership approach relates to the concept and practice of what has come to be known as 'asset-based community development' (ABCD) (Fraser et al, 2014). ABCD describes a panoply of initiatives designed to empower citizens to use their practical skills and social capital to make local improvements in the life of their community. In essence, ABCD represents a strategy for sustainable community development. Its appeal lies in its belief that communities can drive the development process through the identification, mobilisation and valuing of existing (albeit often unrecognised) assets. While the emphasis is on communities, ABCD is as much about mobilising private businesses, public sector agencies, third-sector and voluntary organisations, institutions, associations and other social enterprises in the drive to effectively combine local assets to tackle locally identified problems.

ABCD is attributed to the pioneering work of Kreztmann and McKnight (1993). In their work *Building Communities From the Inside Out: A Path Toward Finding and Mobilizing a Community's Assets* (1993), they distinguish between a 'traditional' approach, described as a 'needs-driven' path (with an emphasis on outside-in definitions of the 'problems' and their solutions) and an alternative asset-based approach. This latter starts instead with an internally focused path; that is, one that is focused on local people, groups and organisations and their existing assets and capacities. Kretzmann and McKnight (1993) outline three basic principles underpinning ABCD:

- It is asset-based, which encompasses the belief in the idea that everyone has something to offer.
- It is internally focused, which advocates the 'inside-out' approach to problem solving rather than an 'outside-in' or 'top-down' approach.
- It is relationship-driven, which means that ABCD thrives on the productive creation of networks, linkages and local capacities.

These asset-based principles seem to correlate with the principles underpinning common understandings of dominant policing orthodoxies, including intelligence-led policing, community policing, problem-oriented policing, neighbourhood policing and community engagement. It also has clear links to the UK Prime Minister David Cameron's (controversial) concept of the 'Big Society' (Cameron,

2010). Table 7.1 below outlines the key features of the needs-based and asset-based approaches.

Table 7.1: Needs-based and asset-based approaches to community development

Needs-based approaches	Asset-based approaches
Starts by looking at a community's deficiencies and problems	Starts by recognising the community's existing capacities and assets (internal focus)
Turns to external agencies (government, charities and so on) to find solutions and achieve change (outside-in approach)	Believes in local people as agents of change in their own lives, with help to self-organise
Tends to characterise people in poverty as victims or passive recipients of help	Sees local people as their own greatest asset and resource in building a stronger community
Can reduce community togetherness as identified problems tend to attract outside resources and professionalised solutions, and brings own pressures where funding is target- or achievement-linked	Encourages collaboration and recognises the process as a journey of discovery (of skills, strengths and how to cooperate); pro-community cohesion
Communities become consumers and clients of services and service providers	Communities become active agents in the co-production of services

Source: Adapted from Church Urban Fund (2013)

It should be noted, of course, that in some respects, the concept of the 'community' as an asset or resource for policing is relatively well established in the literature. In his seminal work on problem-oriented policing (POP), Goldstein (1990) highlights the value of police making more of the community in terms of problem-solving responses (in the specific POP sense, community is defined as 'anyone affected in any way' by the problem under consideration; Goldstein, 1990, p 25.) Elsewhere, the idea of 'co-production' (Ostrom et al, 1978) has been well discussed, and is used to describe a collaborative relationship between service users and service providers particularly as far as the design and delivery of services are concerned.

One example of mobilising community assets can be seen in the public health sector in the UK. Here, a solution has been found whereby patients can find ongoing support through online patient communities such as PatientsLikeMe (see www.patientslikeme.com). This could be adopted to provide a similar scheme for crime victims, whereby victims could access online informal communities or networks of support for as long as they needed following a crime. It is not difficult to see how this idea could be extended beyond existing as a general support network for victims of volume crime, but could be applied to range of community harms (subject to safeguards), including domestic violence and hate crime. In the current policing context, the Gloucestershire Police and Crime Commissioner has included references to ABCD in his *Police and Crime Plan 2013-2017* (Office of the Police and Crime Commissioner Gloucestershire, 2013). As he notes, ABCD is a 'large and growing movement' that considers local assets as the 'building blocks' of sustainable community development supporting safer and stronger communities. Such recognition from within the police service sends encouraging messages about a growing policing awareness of the value of the asset-based approach.

Public involvement

Much of central government's proposals for 'community' crime prevention suggest that voluntary community action should replace collective provision, resulting in a voluntary surveillance society. The extent to which the multi-agency 'call to arms' from both the Home Office Circular 44/90 (Home Office, 1990) and the Morgan report (Home Office, 1991) has affected the thinking, shape and direction of local crime prevention initiatives in the UK is also an important factor. Over the past 20 years, it has become evident that managing criminal acts has become an increasingly diverse problem, with more emphasis on interactive agency work. For Garland (1996), this 'responsibilisation' strategy is a new way of governing crime problems, with the recurring message that the state alone is not, and cannot effectively be responsible for preventing or controlling crime. Others must be made aware that they too have a responsibility in this regard, and have to be persuaded to change their practices in order to reduce criminal opportunities and increase formal controls. In the context of crime prevention, this strategy is clearly associated with the ideas of partnership, multi-agency working and, of course, self-help. In a current context, this approach appears to fit well with the current government's drive for the delivery of public services through the concept of the Big Society, whereby volunteers, charities and others are expected to work closely with partnerships. This is discussed fully elsewhere in this book.

However, as Hughes (2007) pointed out some time ago, there appears very limited evidence in the UK that the bottom-up concerns of multi-layered communities have been of much significance to community safety partnerships, despite Johnston and Shearing (2003) claiming that the partnership approach will lead to a de-monopolisation of expertise and responsibility for crime prevention away from the usual experts.

There is also a well-established body of research since the early days of community safety partnership working that has shown the limits to and problems associated with the approach (Pearson et al, 1992; Crawford, 1997; Hughes, 1996; 1998), with these problems being confirmed by later work of Skinns (2008). Such research should help inform us about future partnerships in terms of plural policing, particularly in the areas of accountability, strategic direction making, organisational culture and information exchange, all of which have been highlighted as problematic within the community safety partnership approach.

Conclusion

The idea of partnership working as a different form of plural policing is a useful one. For the first time, created by an act of parliament, public bodies were required to work together in terms of crime prevention and community safety, with the police as one of the lead organisations. While the approach is not without its problems, it did share the load in terms of service provision, and took away, mainly for the police, the monopolisation of preventative services. However, research also illustrates that when several agencies come together to work on a common cause there are several important areas that need to be considered to ensure the effective delivery of service. These are lessons that need to be understood for the future. In terms of the future of community safety partnerships, it may be that far greater private sector involvement becomes the norm as the concept of private sector involvement in plural policing activities is developed.

Further reading

Goldstein, H. (1990) *Problem-Oriented Policing*, New York, NY: McGraw-Hill.

Hebson, G., Grimshaw, D. and Marchington, M.P. (2003) 'PPPs and the changing public sector ethos: case-study evidence from the health and local authority sectors', *Work, Employment and Society*, vol 17, no 3, pp 481-501.

Home Office (1990) *Circular 44/90, Crime Prevention: The Success of the Partnership Approach*, London: HMSO.

Home Office (1991) *Safer Communities: The Local delivery of Crime Prevention through the Partnership Approach* (Morgan report), London: HMSO.

Home Office (1998) *The Crime and Disorder Act 1998*, London: The Stationery Office.

Home Office (2008) *From the Neighbourhood to the National: Policing our Communities Together*, Cm 7448, London: The Stationery Office.

McLaughlin, E. (2007) *The New Policing*, London: Sage Publications.

Palmiotto, M.J. (2013) *Community Policing: A Police Citizen Partnership*, Abingdon: Routledge.

Rogers, C., (2012) *Crime Reduction Partnerships*, Oxford, Oxford University Press.

Part 3
Consideration of the future

This section considers the potential impact of the concepts surrounding pluralised policing and its practical application in England and Wales, already discussed to some extent in previous chapters. It also examines the foreseeable changes to the public police and to the wider world of plural policing.

For the police organisation itself, reduced budgets and changes in policing philosophy will herald the arrival of completely different role for the police, in terms of its involvement in the delivery of a pluralised policing model. The police organisation could become a relatively minor partner in the delivery of policing to communities, especially at the local level, in contrast to its previous role as prominent partner in many plural policing delivery programmes throughout the country.

In contrast, while the public police change in structure and shape, there is every likelihood that the other constituent organisations that comprise policing could gain momentum as the vacuum left by the public police becomes more apparent. The plural policing world in England and Wales will itself change dramatically in structure and provision in the foreseeable future.

EIGHT

Future directions

Introduction

This chapter consolidates the discussions of previous chapters and considers the future of the police in terms of plurality of policing provision. It considers the way in which the public police are likely to develop over the forthcoming years, and discusses the likely consequences of this. It also considers the implications of a potential situation whereby the public police may be forced to redefine their role based on core issues, thus providing opportunities for the expansion of private provision and other forms of public policing.

Economic framework for change

The police service, like most organisations in the public and private sectors, has been through a period of major challenge and change since the global financial crisis that began in 2008. The government's spending review of 2010 outlined the police service's budget for the following four years. It led to the first significant reduction in police funding and officer numbers in recent history. In 1995/96, total cash funding for the police was £6.2 billion (£9.6 billion in real terms [2014/15 prices]), rising every year to reach £12.9 billion in 2010/11 (£13.8 billion in real terms [2014/15 prices]). Cash funding has fallen in every year since to £11.6 billion in 2015/16 (£11.5 billion in real terms [2014/15 prices]). In March 1995, the total police workforce (officers, police community support officers and staff) numbered 179,900, rising to 243,900 by March 2010. Since then, it has been falling each year, and reached 206,800 in 2015 (rounded full-time equivalent figure) (HMIC, 2015). The police service's performance is most often measured by crime figures, even though these are an incomplete picture of crime and the work carried out by forces. In 1995, 19.1 million offences were committed according to the Crime Survey for England and Wales. This fell in most years to reach 9.3 million offences in 2009/10. The figures have fallen to 6.8 million offences in 2014/15 (HMIC, 2015).

Police forces have been subject to sustained budget reductions since 2010, preceded by a long period of funding increases. Forces have managed this challenge well, making the required spending reductions and balancing their budgets. The total police workforce has fallen by 37,000 between March 2010 and March 2015, with the loss of 16,900 officers, 4,600 police community support officers (PCSOs) and 15,500 police staff. To make these reductions in officer numbers, forces concentrated on reducing or freezing recruitment, rather than losing officers through voluntary severance routes (HMIC, 2015).

Forces have tried to protect the front line as far as possible, and increased the proportion of front-line officers from 89 per cent to 92 per cent between March 2010 and March 2015.

Front-line officers are defined using Her Majesty's Inspectorate of Constabulary's (HMIC's) front-line policing model. This model excludes officers recorded under the 'other' function classification. The 'other' function classification includes police officers on maternity/paternity leave or career break, in full-time education or on suspension, and on long-term leave (sickness, compassionate, special or unpaid) (HMIC, 2014).

By 2014, there were signs that neighbourhood policing was beginning to come under strain as PCSO numbers began to fall. HMIC commented on this in its report *Policing in Austerity: Meeting the Challenge,* published in July 2014. It stated:

> Although we welcome the commitment the service has demonstrated to preserve this vital and fundamental component of our policing model, we remain concerned about the potential erosion of neighbourhood policing. It takes time to build confidence: incremental improvements in confidence at a national level have occurred over a period of almost ten years. The risk is that continuing austerity may put neighbourhood-based proactive and preventative policing in jeopardy. If that happens, the hard-won prize of community confidence could be lost. (HMIC, 2014b)

In spite of the reductions in spending and officer numbers, victims' satisfaction with the service provided by the police remained strong and constant at around 84 per cent each year between 2010/11 and 2014/15 (HMIC, 2014).

During July and August 2015, HMIC carried out a public opinion survey for an inspection, to understand the public's satisfaction with the service provided by their local force as well as to ascertain whether they considered it value for money. The figures showed that most respondents were satisfied with their local police force (52 per cent) compared with 18 per cent who were dissatisfied. Most respondents (65 per cent) perceived no change in the service provided by their local police force over the previous year. A third of respondents (34 per cent) agreed that their local police force offered good value for money, while 19 per cent did not. However, the same survey showed a surprising lack of awareness among the public regarding changes to police funding: only a third of respondents (33 per cent) were aware that police funding had decreased. This is an important point to note, because it affects perceptions of what the police service should be providing for the public.

Despite the fears that there would be major reduction in the comprehensive spending review in the autumn of 2015, this was not the case. It was widely anticipated that cuts ranging from 20 to 50 per cent would be imposed by the government, with police forces being obliged to reconstruct their workforces and their priorities for delivering a service to the public. This fear of budget reduction had some basis. The chief constable of Lancashire Police, for example, publicly stated that his force would not be viable after 2020 if predicted cuts to funding were implemented. He further stated that the changes would introduce a purely reactive force that would respond solely to emergencies, with the effect that mounted sections, dog sections, roads policing teams and community policing teams would disappear (BBC, 2015). This statement was echoed by others; the Merseyside Police and Crime Commissioner, for example, stated that funding reductions would result in the need to cut police, PCSOs and other units, which would have serious repercussions in the area. Forces are still having to carefully manage their resources due to the reductions already imposed by previous cuts to their budgets.

A change in police philosophy?

Van Dijk et al (2015), when discussing the changes seen in the police organisation under austerity and neoliberalist politics, suggest some deep-rooted consequences of such changes that are particularly relevant to the plural world of policing in the future. They suggest that by focusing on two main 'paradigms' of 'control' and 'consent 'at the police institutional level, we are able to effectively analyse these changes.

'Control' is a narrow paradigm in the current analytical context, as it focuses primarily on crime control and maintaining public order through reactive policing, which involves a distance from the public and a disassociation from problem solving and peace keeping. On the other hand, 'consent' is considered to be a broader mandate that seeks approval for its legitimacy from the public, and is more oriented to servicing the community. This involves a wider approach to societal engagement and includes the prevention of crime alongside crime control and public order. The 'control' approach is normally associated with a police system that has a political focus on crime and disorder issues, while the 'consent' approach is most likely found in liberal, democratic societies. Both are reflected in ideological approaches to governance, justice, crime and deviance and the role of policing in society. Choices made at a political level are transmitted in the mandate of the police system through legislation and ministerial guidelines.

In continental Europe, most systems of policing are based on the 'control' paradigm. Here, the police are viewed as an agency of the state or local government; they tend to be distant from the public and devoid of any notion of service. The historical mandate for this approach may be found during the period of Napoleon Bonaparte, whose model for policing the French Empire is seen as the catalyst for later policing models. Central control, maintaining order and forcefully tackling crime suits a conservative world view and mind-set.

On the other hand, the 'consent' paradigm is the model that has been historically utilised in England and Wales, in great contrast to the continental model. Here the primary focus is on crime prevention and preservation of order by consent. This involved a visible police presence on the street by uniformed officers, who were accountable to the law and only allowed to police by consent of the community. There was, in theory at least, independence from central governmental control, with so-called 'operational autonomy' for senior police officers and the much-vaunted 'operational independence' of the police, who are free from political interference. However, this approach may be an ideal type, and is not always fully operated or adhered to at all times and in all places. There may be a gap between rhetoric and reality. For example, with the introduction of Police and Crime Commissioners, the emphasis on reducing crime seems to have gained momentum for chief officers – accountable for their jobs to the Police and Crime Commissioner – at the expense of other factors key to policing by consent. According to Van Dijk and colleagues (2015), this is comparable to the situation of a football manager who is disposable if prizes and wins are not forthcoming.

There may be some substance to the argument surrounding the paradigmatic shift in policing and the role of the police within the new pluralised policing structure. Clearly, the current Home Secretary believes that the function of the police is that of 'cutting crime and only cutting crime' (May, 2010); when this is considered against the reported remarks of David Cameron in 2006 that the police are 'the last great unreformed public service' (Cameron, 2006), it suggests that the move from consent to control is a real one.

In the light of such economic and political changes, how will the police attempt to maintain a viable presence in communities and help protect citizens? There are a number of ideas and initiatives currently being undertaken that may be indicative of the ways in which the police will attempt to maintain their contact with the public in the pluralised policing framework. These are discussed below.

Sponsorship

Sponsorship for specific police functions may be a way forward for the police to at least maintain some elements of their services to the public. In particular, retail associations may be keen to hire police officers for specific patrolling and other duties directly pertaining to the success of their businesses and public peace. For example, in Liverpool, a Business Investment District company that represents more than 1,500 businesses, has apparently agreed to give more funding to Merseyside Police for its officers. The new roles being carried out by the police in this example are additional to current police arrangements, and involve the training of new officers to work directly with the hiring company on a daily basis in the city centre to address such issues as begging, antisocial behaviour and retail crime. Not surprisingly, it has been reported that businesses could now be asked to sponsor Merseyside's mounted section. The practice of hiring police officers for special occasions and functions is not an entirely new one. For many years, football clubs regularly hired police officers from their local force to police football matches and prevent disorderly behaviour. However, the police officers in those circumstances were still accountable to the chief constable for their actions, and it is this area of accountability that may be problematic under a new model of business sponsorship. How do police officers hired by private companies, and engaged in specific duties for those companies, retain their accountability and operational independence when they are being paid for by a body besides the public? It is questions such as these that need to be fully explored if the policing world is to become opened up to the idea of private sponsorship.

In addition, there is the problematic question of deciding who gets 'policed' and why. In this example, there is the danger that those who receive police attention could well be the marginalised, the homeless, the unfortunate and anyone else whom retailers consider bad for business. This raises further questions of accountability and ethical behaviour. Nonetheless, this type of approach may gain momentum if seen as a success from a financial point of view, and will be considered as part of another broad approach to the future, that of collaboration.

Collaboration

A report from the Advisory Group on the National Debate on Policing in Austerity (2015) has considered to some extent what the future of policing should be. It adheres to a clear set of founding principles about policing in the future, citing the policing mission as being to 'prevent crime and protect people from harm'. The suggested framework aims to provide front-line services to communities that include:

- a 24/7 response for both emergencies and non-emergency incidents;
- neighbourhood policing founded on preventative problem solving and community engagement;
- protection through offender management;
- local crime investigations.

These services would be provided collaboratively with other local services involved in community safety. The report also suggests that specialist functions and operational support facilities will be consolidated into cross-force functions, along with greater collaboration through economies of scale for sharing business support functions. While not outright suggesting regionalisation of the 43 police forces in England and Wales, the report does recognise that further development of specialist provisions and functions will be difficult with that number of police forces.

Albeit a useful addition to the debate surrounding the future of the police organisation in England and Wales, the report does tend to ignore the impact of the private sector to a large extent. It appears rooted to the belief that policing activities can only be properly provided by the public police. This to some extent is natural, given that the authors are professionally positioned within the current police service. However, it could be argued that there is some denial by the authors regarding the fact that the public police will be able to carry out these functions outlined in the report, given the enormous reduction in finances and other resources, and an apparent political drive to vastly reduce the numbers of police officers in England and Wales. Nonetheless, the report does raise the question of how the police will be able to effectively work in conjunction with community safety partnerships.

Under sections 22B and 22C of the Police Act 1996, chief constables and Police and Crime Commissioners are under a duty to continually review collaboration opportunities and to ensure that all collaboration is in the interest of the efficiency or effectiveness of their own or other police force areas.

In its report *Policing in Austerity: Meeting the Challenge*, Her Majesty's Inspectorate of Constabulary (HMIC) that collaboration remained disappointing and was "not of the magnitude necessary to meet the requirements of future austerity" (HMIC, 2013). In this report, HMIC found that between 2014/15 and 2018/19, the proportion of net revenue expenditure that is due to be spent on collaborated activity remains broadly stable, at between 14 and 16 per cent.

HMIC found that some forces continued to prioritise force-to-force collaboration, often focused on back-office processes such as human resources and finance. In addition, it focused on those operational services where technical or specialist resources were shared, in order to increase operational resilience or to provide operational support across a geographical area (such as working across different sections of the motorway network). For example, Suffolk and Norfolk Constabularies have established a joint cyber-crime unit in order to tackle the perceived growing threat in both force areas.

A few forces are attempting to expand day-to-day, rather than specialist, operational collaboration. There were impressive and purposeful plans for joint operational working between Cambridgeshire Constabulary, Bedfordshire Police and Hertfordshire Constabulary, where options for a shared public contact function, involving call handling and control rooms, are being developed. Similarly, Thames Valley Police and Hampshire Constabulary have created a single management team for the provision of contact management, as a possible precursor to a fully collaborated unit. (HMIC, 2013).

HMIC found that larger forces tended to doubt the benefit they would derive from force-to-force collaboration in relation to the costs involved, or believed that they would in effect be subsidising smaller forces. Smaller forces were more likely to recognise and realise the benefits of collaboration. There were some regional variations. In the South West, collaboration activity appeared likely to increase significantly with a proposed 'strategic alliance' between Dorset Police and Devon and Cornwall Police, while elsewhere there are plans for greater collaboration between Wiltshire Police and Avon and Somerset Constabulary. In contrast, collaboration between forces in the North

West was comparatively small in scale, focused on operational areas such as organised crime and specialist operational support (for example, motorway policing, firearms operations or dog patrols).

Where collaboration is successful, it relies on forces considering the benefits across all proposed collaboration rather than focusing on deriving direct benefit from each individual area. There are still senior leaders in some forces who refuse to engage in any collaboration programme unless every element of it provides demonstrable savings to their forces. The strongest forces have focused on overall benefit, rather than on the losses or gains from specific parts of the collaboration.

A few forces that are collaborating extensively have found that savings have taken longer to realise than they had hoped. Collaborating forces recognised the need to continue to focus on governance arrangements for collaborative working after the initial structural change. Several commented that it was harder to make major changes to the way in which collaborated units operated compared with areas directly under individual force control. This could mean that forces are less likely to implement major changes to improve the efficiency of already collaborated units (HMIC, 2013).

HMIC found that some forces were focusing on expanding collaborative working with blue-light and other services within the force boundary, rather than on force-to-force collaboration. Forces were increasingly sharing information or becoming involved in joint working with other organisations, utilising such platforms as the so-called multi-agency safeguarding hubs or community safety teams. Some forces are now adopting a more structured approach to collaboration with local partners, either through combining, or looking to combine, their estates (HMIC, 2013).

Meanwhile, other forces have chosen to continue to build on collaborations with local councils. For example, Hampshire Constabulary has formed a partnership with Hampshire County Council and the Hampshire Fire and Rescue Service to provide all human resources, finance and administrative services to the force. HMIC believes that, while collaboration is not the only or the most important tool available to forces to meet their budget reductions, it continues to be a valuable option, and, given the statutory duty to explore and adopt collaboration, there remains considerable scope for forces to pursue it further.

Changes in police education and recruitment

The College of Policing, in a recent report on future demand for services from the police (College of Policing, 2015a), illustrates very clearly the way in which calls for police action are changing, and will continue to change, in the near future. Traditional acquisitive crime is falling, while information-based crime, such as internet fraud and crimes targeting the vulnerable, are on the increase. New offences require different expertise and skill sets, and necessitate greater levels of cross-organisational working and leadership. Reduction in numbers of police staff is linked to several factors, including the increase in specialist departments, the decline of general patrol and a move to professionalise police officers through a degree programme. The College of Policing (2015a) also highlights the fact that the number of police officers in England and Wales has been falling over the past five years. As police officers and staff numbers decline, there is concern about whether forces will be able to maintain levels of service delivery. This report indicates that the proportion of adults who reported seeing a police officer on foot patrol in their local area at least once a week fell from 38 per cent in 2011/12 to 34 per cent in 2012/13. Clearly, the police service of the future will be leaner, and have more specialist officers and departments with possibly little visible general patrol functions. Consequently, we may need a new type of police officer, one with more pronounced leadership and professional abilities than hitherto required.

Degree entry?

The College of Policing (College of Policing, 2016) has recently announced a consultation process in order to make the police organisation a degree-entry profession, which means that there are certain requirements that need to be met. These include:

- a specialist knowledge base;
- a distinct ethical dimension;
- continuous professional development;
- standards of education and accreditation.

While the police service in England and Wales, under the guidance of the College of Policing, is in the process of developing the first three aspects of professionalism listed, the fourth element of education and accreditation needs further.refinement. Consequently, at the 2015 annual conference of Excellence in Policing , the problem surrounding inconsistencies in police training and education were discussed. Producing better, professional leaders is considered to be one way in which the police service may adjust to and perform well in the new pluralised world of policing. Dame Shirley Pearce (2015) suggests that there are three types of variable that are currently undermining the police service and need to be addressed. These are:

- The discrepancy in the way in which police officers are selected, as forces have individualised selection processes and entry requirements This ranges from no specific qualifications being required to the expected completion of a foundation degree. This means there are large differences in knowledge and experience amongst constables.
- A lack of consistent approach to further training or accreditation of officers once they are selected. Skills learned in one force are not necessarily recognised by another force, with consequent retraining needed for police officers.
- The need for new and specialist skills to deal with changing patterns of crime, with greater clarity on the skills needed for new and specialist staff in important positions. National training standards that are consistent are important for the future of the police.

Speaking at the same conference, Peach (2015) outlined a new framework that involves working with universities and the higher education sector to allow officers to undertake self-funded undergraduate degree programmes or police force-funded merger programmes. The aim is to end the discrepancies that exist as result of some forces recruiting graduates and working with universities on training, and others struggling to recruit officers with three diplomas or other equivalents to A levels, and finding the development of further training for these officers a challenge. Pointing to the fact that approximately 42 per cent of the population is educated to degree level, and with European police forces moving towards a graduate workforce, Peach suggested it was time for degree-level training to take a more prominent place in policing in England and Wales.

In response to these recommendations, the College of Policing has suggested two graduate-level routes into policing: a full degree combined with the later development of skills by working in conjunction with both the force and the university, or a conversion programme, similar to a postgraduate certificate, for those who have completed another degree. For superintendents, there are a number of questions being considered, including whether any master's degree is suitable for policing or whether it should be in a relevant subject from an agreed list, or an entirely bespoke programme. In addition to increased educational qualifications, the police service in England and Wales would retain its enhanced entry provisions, such as the recently introduced fast-track and direct-entry programmes, in its drive to become more professional.

Fast-track and direct-entry programmes

The fast-track and direct-entry programmes have been designed to open up entry to the service to talented individuals from diverse backgrounds, with the aim of bringing new perspectives to support the continuous development of policing. As well as attracting, identifying and developing the most talented constables, it also looks to recruit special constables and police staff from within the police service (College of Policing, 2015b).

The fast-track entry scheme offers a development programme and promotion mechanism to enable the most talented to advance more rapidly to the rank of inspector (within two years for serving constables and three years for police staff, special constables and external graduates). This will enable the service to develop a cadre of officers with the skills, experience and capacity to reach the senior ranks of the service – at least that of superintendent – to have an impact on and positively influence the management and culture of policing.

The direct-entry programme at superintendent level supports the national policing vision in helping to bring existing exceptional leaders into the police service to have an immediate impact on culture, efficiency and effectiveness. This will be achieved by opening up entry to the service to proven leaders who will join policing directly at the rank of superintendent, rather than having to work their way up from the rank of constable. Programme members will be trained over 18 months and given coaching and mentoring, to equip them with the skills required to perform as superintendents who inspire confidence in officers, staff and the public. This will create a cohort that has the potential to further develop and acquire the skills and experience to progress to the chief officer ranks.

In the future, the College of Policing is proposing to consolidate direct entry schemes with three other entry points to become a police officer. These are:

- an undergraduate degree in policing;
- a graduate conversion programme;
- higher-level apprenticeships.

While these proposals are currently undergoing consolidation and are far from being completed, they clearly demonstrate a drive for a new form of professionalisation.

Increased reliance on technology

As technology in its various forms becomes more widespread, the police will seek to use it in the belief that it will make them far more economical, efficient and ultimately effective. The process of bringing the police force up to date with current technological developments has accelerated enormously in recent years, with police officers now utilising hand-held devices that mean they are able to undertake record keeping and incident reporting at the scene of an incident rather than having to attend a police station to fill in forms. It is believed that the introduction and use of body-worn cameras seen elsewhere in the world will soon become the norm in the UK, not just to protect the rights of citizens but also to persuade individuals to plead guilty in court by providing recorded evidence gained from the incident contemporaneously, thereby obviating police officers from attending court and allowing them to remain active on the street.

Other forms of technology designed to replace the human face of the police officer while providing a practical service will be introduced. The current police preoccupation with the use of drones for specific activities is likely to increase as the utility and cost-effectiveness of such devices are more firmly established. Drones can be used for searching wide areas for missing persons and can be used to undertake activities that may be harmful to human beings, as well as being useful for general surveillance activities.

Cambridgeshire Police are currently trialling the use of Skype as a means to free up officer time for neighbourhood patrols and offer more flexibility for victims, who are to be encouraged to contact and speak to the police via the free online communication tool rather than using traditional methods of communication, meaning an officer may not need to attend the scene of an incident. The Police Federation, however, has raised concerns about those people unable to use or afford to pay for the technology required for this type of online audio-visual call system. Despite the claim of the Cambridgeshire force that the Skype method will provide greater flexibility for victims as well as allowing better response times, the Home Office has stated it would be up to other individual forces to decide whether or not to adopt a similar approach.

In addition to the use of this type of technology, other forces are working collaboratively to use private security assistance. The Leicestershire, Nottinghamshire and Northamptonshire forces have asked private provider G4S to carry out a feasibility study to see what it might be able to offer. The idea is apparently to allow the three forces to gain information about what G4S might be able to offer in terms of service delivery, in areas such as contact management whereby the public contact the police for help and assistance. But Unison, the union for civilian staff, has voiced concerns about the collaboration, as union membership and the security of members' jobs may be affected if such an initiative results in police numbers being cut and G4S posts being paid at a lower rate.

However, greater use of technology brings with it inherent problems, despite being a potential source of change for the police. The general aim of most of the technology being discussed for future use revolves around the minimisation of contact time between the community member, be they a victim of crime or otherwise, and the police. The oft-used term 'free up officers' time' suggests that police will therefore become more efficient and effective. However, such a lack of contact necessitates a reduction in police visibility and social interaction within a community, and this can be a negative aspect. We saw in Chapter One how the democratic policing model in the UK depends on the role and support of the community. This support is provided because the public, in the main, believe in the police and the methods they employ. Tyler (2003) refers to the role of procedural justice, a key aspect of which is the ethical, fair and transparent methods used by an accountable police organisation. This is fundamental to the process of the police and community working together. There is a clear danger, as the police withdraw to 'core values' and, to use Van Dijk and colleagues' (2015) phrase, retreat to a 'control model', that the gains made by generations of interaction between police and communities could be seriously damaged. This damage would only be enhanced if underpinned by a large upsurge in the use of technology that distances the police from the community. The public's belief in the legitimacy and authority of the police could be thus damaged, undermining a policing model that is still viewed with envy across the world.

Other challenges

For the police of the future, the pluralised world of provision will become even more of a reality. Cultural beliefs and stereotypes regarding other forms of policing are already under challenge, and the reality could be that in terms of day-to-day policing provision, the public police will have much more limited involvement. Police officers may instead become more specialised in their duties and we may see the introduction of the 'armchair detective', dealing with IT-related crime through the use of computer systems and technology. Certainly, there will need to be a certain number of police officers employed to exercise their powers of arrest and so on when needed, but these could become drastically reduced, especially if such bodies as police and PCSOs are granted further powers.

The changes envisioned for the delivery of policing by the public police, in conjunction with other agencies and volunteers, of course raises other important issues. Perhaps the most important is that of accountability. Questions remain concerning how pluralised policing activities can be monitored, with many different organisations involved at the delivery stage. How will transparency be maintained, with perhaps several different types of accountability processes – both public and private – coexisting?

Historically, the police service has lacked reliable data to allow forces to monitor, describe and predict how demand for services changes over time. This lack of information represents a weakness for the police service in terms of robust planning for the future, and has resulted in levels of recorded crime becoming a proxy measure for police workload.

The police deal with a wide range of what are sometimes referred to as 'non-crime incidents' that are not captured as part of recorded crime levels – 84 per cent of all command and control calls relate to 'non-crime incidents'. Much of the police activity that results from these calls relates to issues of vulnerability, public protection and safeguarding. As with crimes that relate to vulnerability, these incidents are likely to be complex, with many involving combined organisational responses including those of mental health services, for example. In addition to these statutory responsibilities, the police are becoming increasingly involved in other protective activities to prevent the re-victimisation of vulnerable people, including multi-agency risk assessment conferences and troubled family interventions. In summary:

- Demands on the police associated with protective statutory requirements, such as multi-agency public protection panels, appears to be increasing.
- There is a continued requirement for all forces to meet national obligations and standards, including those set out in the so-called Strategic Policing Requirement and in relation to specialist areas

of policing such as counter-terrorism, organised crime and public order.

As part of a recent report, the National Audit Office (Morse, 2015) examined whether the Home Office, along with other policing stakeholders, had effectively managed the risks of reduced police funding. The report concluded that most forces do not have a thorough evidence-based understanding of demand, which makes it difficult for them to transform services intelligently and demonstrate they are achieving value for money. The ACPO advisory group on police finances agrees with this analysis. The NAO report went on to conclude that the Home Office needs to be better informed in order to discharge its ultimate responsibility for overseeing the police, distributing funding and assuring parliament that forces are indeed providing value for money. The report states that the Home Office needs to work with HMIC, the College of Policing, Police and Crime Commissioners and police forces to fill the significant gaps in understanding demand, and to be able to better identify those occasions when forces may be at risk of failing to meet the policing needs of local communities.

It would be wrong and misleading to think about the future of policing solely in terms of the activities carried out by the public police. Crawford (2014) predicts that the future of policing will be one of pluralised provision, which will be multi-faceted and will involve changes inside and outside of the police organisation. Having considered the potential changes affecting the public police, the next section examines the possible developments in store for those other actors involved in the delivery of plural policing, including providers of private security provision, volunteers such as the special constabulary, and PCSOs. It also briefly discusses implications for the accountability of local policing.

Private security provision

In June 2012, David Taylor-Smith, the head of G4S in the UK and Africa, predicted that private companies would be running large parts of the British police service within five years. This would, he argued, be driven by a combination of budgetary pressure and political will (Taylor and Travis, 2012). Despite the various problems and perceived deceleration of the privatisation implementation in 2012, when G4S announced its inability to meet the terms of its £284 million contract with the government (Crawford, 2014), this has not signalled the end of private security involvement in the delivery of policing.

There are clear indications that the process will continue, and is likely to gather pace as new economic constraints are introduced into the police service as well as other public agencies. Clearly, this will involve the need to persuade the public that policing provision can be supplied by others besides the traditional, public police organisation. This may not be as difficult as previously thought. Jones and Newburn (2002a) believe that the current state of plural policing in England and Wales is not a break with the past but represents continuity with, and a formulation of, a continuum of social control. For example, groups like the 'thief-takers' and other commercial organisations maintained order in the 18th century in London (Tobias, 1979). An example of this continuity with historic forms of social control is the Thames River Police, founded as a privately funded police force in the late 18th century as a means to combat theft of cargo from the pool of London. These independent and privately funded forms of policing illustrate the fact that the plural policing approach has a long history.

The growth of private security provision across the globe echoes the situation in England and Wales. For example, the United Nations Office on Drugs and Crime (UNODC) highlights that the industry in France has grown from 100,000 personnel in 1982 to 160,000 in 2011, while in Japan the equivalent figure rose from 70,000 in 1975 to 460,000 in 2003. In India, there exist over 7 million private security personnel, outnumbering police officers 4.98 to one (UNODC, 2011).

Further, there are examples in England and Wales of a more widespread acceptance of private security personnel's role in providing security and safety, especially in the absence of the public police at a local level. In Frinton-on-Sea in Essex, which has 4,000 residents but no police station and just six PCSOs who must travel around by bus or bike, residents pay £100 each a year for a private security film to patrol their streets because of an evident lack of public police (Fritton, 2015). The residents pay the security company AGS to patrol the town by car every night between 7pm and 7am, as well as to provide an emergency phone line, although they still call 999 if the situation is serious. Despite criticism that this heralds a two-tier system of policing, residents appear happy to pay for the service, despite the fact that the security personnel have no more powers than the average citizen's arrest. However, they are perceived as being a deterrent for potential criminals, with their presence also providing some reassurance for residents in the area. The firm charges each resident £2 per week for its services and employs three individuals in two vehicles, which apparently look similar to police cars, to carry out patrols. Each individual wears a uniform similar to that worn by police officers, and they also wear body cameras.

In a similar vein, the village of Tiptree in Essex (Tiptree, 2015) is planning to hire its own private security team to tackle a perceived crime wave, after the local police force stated its intention to get rid of beat officers. It has been reported that burglaries in this area have risen 250 per cent over the past 12 months, and incidents of antisocial behaviour and other criminal activity have also increased. However, Essex Police says that it no longer has the resources to react to low-level crimes or isolated incidents. Parish councillors decided to take action after learning further that PCSOs would no longer be available from April 2016. The village had already lost its dedicated police officers and the police station was closed in 2011; as a result, local councillors voted to consider increasing the precept paid by the 9,000 residents to cover the cost of security staff and a warden. The perceived advantages of this approach were quoted as being that the security firm would patrol the area in the evenings, when most of the trouble seemed to occur. While the private security staff would not have the powers to detain or arrest, they would become more effective under the introduction of a community safety accreditation scheme, which could give public, private or voluntary sector staff limited powers including that of issuing penalty notices for minor offences.

Local politicians are concerned by this trend of communities paying for private security, urging instead that a rise in council tax should be introduced to assist in funding the public police. They suggest that an extra 50p per week per resident would be sufficient to fund 300 extra officers in Essex working on behalf of the whole community, not merely those who can afford and are prepared to pay considerably more for private security provision. It is estimated that Essex Police needs to save £60 million over the next five years due to budget cuts.

Elsewhere, there have been instances whereby communities have attempted to self-fund policing, such as in Upton Grey and the Candovers (Brown Candover and Chilton Candover) in Hampshire, where residents suggested that the community pay £60,000 for each of the next three years to keep a dedicated beat officer on their streets. However, the local Police and Crime Commissioner rejected the idea, stating that police provision had to be 'equitable'. In May, it emerged that villagers in the Essex village of Tolleshunt D'Arcy were patrolling the neighbourhood themselves in an effort to stem a perceived flood of crime in their isolated community.

What these examples illustrate is that there is an appetite among communities to seek private security provision as a replacement for the public police at the local level, and smaller private security companies appear to be especially popular in this regard. However, these examples also illustrate that opening up the marketplace for security and safety provision may well reinforce the inequalities inherent in our society, with those not being able to pay for such provision more likely to become victims of crime and disorder.

Clearly, the role of the private sector is likely to increase as police managers attempt to cut costs and make efficiency savings. However, the appetite for private security solutions is unlikely to be replicated in other European countries, where there is little support for private security to become involved in what is considered to be a fundamental function of the state. Despite this, the momentum to utilise more and more private security arrangements in the delivery of policing at a local level in England and Wales will only increase in scope and volume in the foreseeable future.

Special constables

The College of Policing's leadership review (College of Policing, 2015b) recognised that special constables were well integrated into many areas of policing, but, in respect of their leadership responsibilities, there persists an 'us and them' mentality. Special constables have a hierarchy, but that hierarchy is not integrated into the regular service. The review concluded that, given the wealth of leadership skills and capability among 'specials', this group should have the supervisory powers and responsibilities of regular officers, provided that they meet the same standards. In practice, this would align policing more closely with the operation of reservists in the armed forces, who are selected for their competence and developed to have the command and supervisory responsibilities of that rank regardless of whom they are leading.

If policing adopts such an approach, it would enable special constables to be linked to other leadership review recommendations, which would, for instance, create a new model of leadership and management training and development (recommendation 6), introduce national standards for recruitment and promotion (recommendation 9), and examine the implications of exit and re-entry into policing (recommendation 4).

Police community support officers

Despite the perceived usefulness of PCSOs and a belief that they may play an enhanced role in future local policing initiatives, fears have been expressed about the future of their neighbourhood policing role. This is because the police need to cut substantial amounts of money from their budget. In Devon and Cornwall, for example, 1,300 jobs, including 760 police officers and all 360 PCSOs in the region, could be lost.

In London, some boroughs are also considering the removal of PCSOs completely, as there is doubt regarding the sustainability of the current level of policing provision. Fuelling this uncertainty are potential plans to completely remove PCSOs from the policing landscape more generally across the UK. For example, the 16 wards in the borough of Kingston are currently policed by 22 PCSOs working in teams of two or three (Kingston, 2015), but it is suspected that the majority of jobs lost in the borough will be those of PCSOs.

Just as traffic wardens (originally police employees) became the responsibility of local authorities and private companies, so too could the work of other police staff following the Lincolnshire experiment. Here, former police staff have been transferred to a private company. PCSOs could be in line for similar private management, especially if their role and function cannot be maintained under future plans for the provision of policing.

Community volunteers

In England and Wales, there are over 10,000 police support volunteers, participating actively in policing and in providing services to their communities that police forces do not have the capability or capacity to provide. In support of sustaining such an environment of volunteering, the College of Policing concluded in its leadership review (2015b) that volunteers could be more engaged in providing leadership within the service. Findings suggested that there are a relatively limited number of volunteers who are given supervisory or managerial responsibilities, for which cultural and organisational issues within policing are likely to be responsible. The philosophy is very different within other organisations, such as the National Trust and many other charities whose volunteers are actively encouraged to lead teams or occupy positions of responsibility in the delivery of key services. It would not be not be appropriate to use volunteers in every policing role, but for some functions, especially those involving the supervision of other volunteers or the management of community-based or less time-critical services, there is scope for developing a bigger cohort of volunteer managers in policing.

The current government's view appears to be that while the office of constable is central to the delivery of policing in England and Wales, there are opportunities for the role to be enhanced by others, including police staff and volunteers. Consequently, there is an ongoing consultation regarding the way in which chief officers designate powers (Home Office, 2015). There appears to be a belief that volunteers currently undertaking such roles as working at police enquiry desks or giving crime prevention advice could potentially offer so much more to the police service. Thus, the government is keen to encourage those volunteers with specific skill sets to become more involved in helping the police investigate specific criminal activity; volunteers with specialist IT or accountancy skills, for example, may be asked to assist with the investigation of cyber or financial crime. As their experience grows, their skills will ultimately enable them to play a greater part in investigations.

Individuals wishing to volunteer their time to policing currently have two choices. They may either become special constables with a full range of powers, or they can become police support volunteers, a supporting role in the main, with very few powers attached. Reforming the powers of volunteers was recognised by the College of Policing in its leadership review (College of Policing, 2015b). In particular, the following recommendations were made:

• Recommendation 7: increase flexibility in assigning powers and legal authorities to staff.
• Recommendation 8: develop career opportunities that allow recognition and reward for advanced practitioners.

The government is of the view that there are currently barriers that deter people from contributing their time and expertise to helping keep their communities safe. They point to the example of special constables and argue that the particular low regard for and low status of this role, which confers on practitioners the same powers as regular officers and carries the expectation that they will intervene in situations when not on duty, is something that may deter applicants from volunteering The future could see chief officers having the ability to designate volunteers to carry out certain tasks normally reserved for sworn officers; this would, it is argued, help them shape their workforce in the way that they need to police their force areas as effectively as possible. It may also enable individuals to volunteer for roles that interest them and allow these individuals to use their skills to serve the community, where previously the community may have missed out on their services. The example used by the Home Office to support its argument in favour of reforming volunteer powers is that of Lincolnshire Police, which has already trained and deployed a number of volunteer PCSOs to the same standard as their paid PCSOs, albeit the former currently have no powers as the law does not permit it.

The government further argues that its proposals have the potential to affect the police and other law enforcement agencies in that chief officers will be able to deliver a number of services using staff and volunteers rather than officers, which is likely to save thousands of hours of police officer time that could be more effectively used. However, delivering training to new volunteers and issuing them with uniforms means that police forces will incur some costs. Moreover, the advantages and disadvantages are all based the assumption that community members will actually volunteer in sufficient numbers to have an impact on the work required in the pluralised world of policing.

Table 8.1: Current position of paid staff and volunteers

	Full powers	Some powers	No powers
Paid, full-time or part-time staff	Police officer	Designated staff (PCSO, investigating officer, detention/escort officer)	Other police staff
Unpaid part-time staff	Special constable	No current role	Police support volunteers

Source: Home Office (2015)

Future accountability

Accepting the future as one of pluralised delivery involving several different agencies and interested parties has its challenges, particularly in terms of the organisation and accountability of such a pluralised delivery approach. A theoretical model of local policing has been suggested in this book (see Chapter Three), but just how this would be regulated is open to discussion. One solution could be that of a regional policing body that would oversee cross-border delivery and cooperation, as well as focusing on accountability at the local community level.

When discussing the joint delivery of policing, both at the international and national level, Stenning and Shearing (2015) believe that most organisations engaged in private provision share the same general orientations of crime control through law enforcement as their state-based counterparts. This would suggest that bodies of private and public provision actually have much in common, and that accountability processes could be similar for both types of provision. Stenning and Shearing (2015) further suggest that the system of locally elected Police and Crime Commissioners (PCCs) has been introduced in England and Wales to replace police authorities, which were previously responsible for governing local police services, so it is perhaps to the PCCs themselves that we must turn to provide the organisation and regulation of locally defined plural policing. This may be easier than at first considered, due to the fact that PCCs' legal and financial responsibilities include locating community safety partnerships funding, and ensuring that special grants, such as drugs grants and other forms of income generation such as the night-time economy levy, are utilised effectively, as well as setting annual budgets (Rogers and Gravelle, 2012) The PCC's role is much more extensive than responsibility for the police service, so there is every possibility that, given the current economic pressures and changes to the police organisation itself, alternative sources of security, such as private delivery, may become attractive to PCCs. While acknowledging that PCCs may not currently be in the best position to oversee and regulate policing provision involving a myriad of agencies, Crawford (2014) suggests that any future reform in this area must include powers to regulate and oversee the plurality of policing provision.

Conclusion

Roycroft (2014) might be slightly optimistic in his view that continuing to streamline service provision, with both the specialist and backroom functions of the police being improved, is the way forward in police reform. Rather, perhaps, we may see a further reduction in the numbers of sworn officers, in favour of a large share of social control at the local level being enforced through methods involving citizen participation and engagement. This approach will be supported in the main by private contracts, with formal sworn policing occasionally being introduced as and when it is required. In fact, Bayley and Shearing (1996) suggest that sworn or warranted police should concentrate on law enforcement, and leave crime prevention and community safety functions to municipal and commercial bodies.

It seems unlikely that the core principles of policing will change in the future. The police will always be expected to prevent or respond to crime, harmful acts and accidents, both as an emergency service and as the primary organisation charged with preventing and investigating crime. But the policing mission has also widened to include greater provision for the vulnerable, for people's safety in private and public spaces, and increasingly online. Leaders in police and partner organisations must find more effective ways to deal with the demands of the digitally enabled, globally connected world.

The trends and challenges identified in any horizon scanning suggest that the police and their partners must find ways of empowering individuals to contribute to collective efforts, adapt to different situations and improve the flow of information and decision making throughout the chain of command. This means a more professional approach from all members of the police service. The future context in which the police will operate may see forces taking responsibility for work delivered by multidisciplinary teams or managing and being managed by people from other sectors, and we can expect to see more movement by choice in and out of the police service at different levels. This requires alliances to be forged and the use of influence and persuasion, as well as the development of an increasingly collective leadership ethos based on the recognition that tough problems require whole systems to help solve them.

There is no escaping the fact that the face of public policing will change dramatically over the next decade or so. Claims that the UK has a fully integrated democratic policing model, working through community to solve problems, will be challenged. Neighbourhood policing teams, for example, often seen as the manifestation of the community policing approach in England and Wales, will change to such an extent that they will either be non-existent or will be required to cover such a large geographical area that their effectiveness may be called into question.

There would appear to be large structural changes ahead for the police organisation; as such, the current 43 police forces in England and Wales may not be tenable for the future. Collaboration and outsourcing, with forces jointly working together, could inevitably lead to the creation of a more regional approach to the delivery of policing services. The police as an organisation will become leaner, with vastly reduced numbers of officers. However, those officers will become more professional, possibly educated to degree level across the force, with a greater reliance on technology than ever before to assist them in their duties. Specialisms will continue to develop as new crimes become more prominent, especially crimes involving IT and cyberspace, and randomised foot or vehicle patrol by the public police will likely become a thing of the past.

Reiner (2007) sees the recent changes to law and order, and of course policing, as part of a broader shift of responsibility for security and welfare from government to private citizens, a core feature of the neoliberal approach discussed earlier in this work, which increases profitability for private companies with the cost being the reduction of collective responsibility. Indeed, for Sklansky (2008), the challenge posed by the continued unfettered growth of private policing provision is that it would diminish the level and perhaps the quality of services available to those less able to pay.

Whatever the reality of the political and economic situation we now find ourselves in, one thing is certain. The future of policing provision in England and Wales is undergoing, and will continue to undergo, significant changes as it makes the transition from state-owned provision to a plural and multifaceted provision of services to the community.

Further reading

BBC (2015a) 'Lancashire Police not viable by 2020', available at www.bbc.co.uk/news/uk-England-Lancashire-34503004 (accessed 25 November 2015).

BBC (2015b) 'Lincolnshire Police and G4S improving services', available at www.bbc.co.uk/news/uk-34864781 (accessed 26 November 2015).

Bayley, D.H. and Shearing, C.D. (2005) 'The future of policing', in T. Newburn (ed) *Policing: Key Readings*, Cullompton: Willan.

Blair, I. (2003) 'Leading towards the future', Paper presented at the Future of Policing Conference, London School of Economics, 10 October, www.padpolice.com/futureofpolicing.php (accessed 21 July 2015).

College of Policing (2015) 'Leadership review', available at www.college.police.uk/What-we-do/Development/Promotion/the-leadership-review/Documents/Leadership_Review_Final_June-2015.pdf (accessed 17 November 2015).

Crawford, A. (2014) 'Police, policing and the future of the policing family', in J.M. Brown (ed) *The Future of Policing*, Abingdon: Routledge.

Gibbs, B. and Greenhalgh, B., (2014) 'The police mission in the twenty first century: rebalancing the role of the first public service', available at www.no-offence.org/pdfs/69.pdf (accessed 22 November 2015).

Home Office (2015) 'Reforming the powers of police staff and volunteers', available at

www.gov.uk/government/uploads/system/uploads/attachment_data/
  file/459450/150909_Consultation_Document_on_Powers_of_
  Police_Staff_and_Volunteers__FINAL_.pdf (accessed 17 November
  2015).

Independent Police Commission (2013) *Policing for a Better Britain:
  Report of the Independent Police Commission*, London: Independent
  Police Commission.

IFS (Institute for Fiscal Studies) (2015) 'The IFS green budget',
  available at
www.ifs.org.uk/events/1110.

Lister, S. and Jones, T. (2015) 'Plural policing and the challenge
  of democratic accountability', in S. Lister and M. Rowe (eds)
  Accountability of Policing, Abingdon: Routledge.

  Morse, A. (2015) *Financial sustainability of police forces in England and
  Wales*, London: Home Office.

  National Debate Advisory Group (2015) 'Reshaping policing for
  the public', available at www.npcc.police.uk/documents/reports/
  Reshaping%20policing%20for%20the%20public.pdf (accessed 9
  November 2015).

  Prenzler, T. (2013) *Outsourcing of Policing Tasks: Scope and Prospects*,
  Sydney: Australian Security Industry.

  Taylor, M. and Travis, A. (2012) 'G4S chief predicts mass police
  privatisation', www.theguardian.com/uk/2012/jun/20/g4s-chief-
  mass-police-privatisation (accessed 16 November 2015).

  White, A. (2015) 'The politics of police privatisation: a multiple
  streams approach', *Criminology and Criminal Justice*, vol 15, no 3, pp
  283-99.

References

ACPO (Association of Chief Police Officers) (2005) *Practice Advice on Core Investigative Doctrine 2005*, Cambridge: NCPE.

ACPO (2006) *Practice Advice on Professionalising the Business of Neighbourhood Policing*, Wyboston: Centrex.

ADT (2006) *Anti-social behaviour across Europe*. Sunbury-on-Thames: ADT. Available at: http://www.adt.pt/informacao-corporativa/ AntiSocialBehavioUrAcrossEurope_EN.pdf. (Accessed 14 July 2016)

Allison, R (2000) 'Doctor driven out of home by vigilantes', *The Guardian* [online]. Available from: http://www.guardian.co.uk/ uk/2000/aug/30/childprotection.society. (Accessed 14 July 2016).

Bang, H. (2005) 'Among everyday makers and expert citizens', in J. Newman (ed) *Remaking Governance*, Bristol: Policy Press, pp 159-79.

BBC (2010) 'David Cameron launches Tories' "Big Society" plan', http://www.bbc.co.uk/news/uk-10680062, (Accessed accessed [26/08/ August 2010).

BBC (2015a), 'Lancashire Police not viable by 2020', available at available at http://www.bbc.co.uk/news/uk-England-Lancashire-34503004 (Accessed accessed 25/11/ November 2015).

BBC (2015b) 'Lincolnshire Police and G4S improving services', available at available at http://www.bbc.co.uk/news/uk-34864781 (Accessed accessed 26 November 2015/11/15).

Bayley, D.H and Shearing, C.D (1996) 'The future of policing', *Law and Society Review*, vol 30, no 3, pp 585-606.

Bayley, D.H. and Shearing, C.D. (2005) 'The future of policing', in T. Newburn (ed), *Policing: Key Readings*, Cullompton: Willan.

Bayley, D.H and Shearing, C.D (1996) 'The Future of Policing', *Law and Society Review*, vol 30, no 3, pp 585-606.

Benn, S. I. and Gaus, G.F. (1983) *Public and Private in Social Life*, London: Croom Helm.

Berkley, G.E. (1969) *The Democratic Policeman*, Boston, MA: Beacon Press.

Berry, G., Izat, J., Mawby, R., Walley, L. and Wright, A. (1998) *Practical Police Management*, London: Police Review Publishing Co.

Berry, J. (2007) 'Officer numbers could be slashed', available at www.policemag.co.uk/Archive/2006/0606/0606.pdf (accessed 26 November 2015).

Bittner, E. (ed) (1970) *The Functions of the Police in Modern Society*, Cambridge, MA: Oelgeschlager, Gunn and Hain Publishers.

Blair, I. (2003) 'Leading towards the future', Paper presented at the Future of Policing Conference, LSE, 10 October, www.padpolice.com/futureofpolicing.php, accessed 21 July 2015.

Brown, C. (1997) *Dwelling Burglaries: The Need for Multi Agency Strategies*, Police Research Group, London: Home Office.

Bullock, K. (2014) *Citizens, Community and Crime Control*, Basingstoke: Palgrave Macmillan.

Bullock, K. and Sindall, K. (2014) 'Examining the nature and extent of public participation in neighbourhood policing', *Policing and Society*, vol 24, no 44, pp 385-404.

Butler, P. (2015) 'Why the "big society" is now just a hashtag for coalition hypocrisy', available at www.theguardian.com/profile/patrickbutler (accessed 22 March 2016).

Button. M. (2002) *Private Policing*, Cullompton: Willan.

Cabinet Office (2010) *Building the Big Society*, London: Cabinet Office

Caless, B. (2007) '"Numties in yellow jackets": the nature of hostility towards the Police Community Support Officer in Neighbourhood Policing Teams', *Policing*, vol 1, no 2, pp 187-95.

Cameron, D. (2006) 'The police are the last great unreformed public service', available at www.telegraph.co.uk/comment/personal-view/3622123/Daddy-Cameron-knows-whats-best.html, accessed 26 November 2015.

Cameron, D. (2010) Big Society Speech, Liverpool, July 19 Available at http://www.number10.gov.uk/news/speeches-and-transcripts/2010/07/big-society-speech-53572 (accessed 14 July 2016).

Casey, L. (2008) *Engaging communities in fighting crime*, London: Cabinet Office.

Church Urban Fund (2013) *Tackling Poverty in England: An Asset-Based Approach*, Church Urban Fund: London.

Cohen, S. (1985) *Visions of Social Control*, Cambridge: Polity Press.

College of Policing (2015a) 'Estimating demand on the police service', available at www.college.police.uk/News/College-news/Documents/Demand%20Report%2023_1_15_noBleed.pdf (accessed November 2015).

College of Policing (2015b) 'Leadership review', available at www.college.police.uk/What-we-do/Development/Promotion/the-leadership-review/Documents/Leadership_Review_Final_June-2015.pdf (accessed 17 November 2015).

College of Policing (2016) 'Consultation document on qualification framework', available at www.college.police.uk/What-we-do/Learning/Policing-Education-Qualifications-Framework/Documents/PEQF_consultation_final_290116.pdf (accessed 22 March 2016).

Commission of the European Communities, (2004), Brussels, available at http://ec.europa.eu/information_society/doc/qualif/health/COM_2004_0356_F_EN_ACTE.pd

Cooper, C., Anscombe, J., Avenell, J., McLean, F. and Morris, J. (2006) 'A national evaluation of community support officers, available at http://socialwelfare.bl.uk/subject-areas/services-activity/criminal-justice/homeoffice/141516hors297.pdf (accessed 21 March 2016).

Corvellec, H. (2009) 'The practice of risk management: silence is not absence', *Risk Management: An International Journal*, vol 11, no 304, pp 285-304.

Cosgrove, F.M. (2016) '"I wanna be a copper": the engagement of police community support officers with the dominant police occupational culture', *Criminology and Criminal Justice*, vol 16, no 1, pp 119-38.

Crawford, A. (1997) *The Local Governance of Crime: Appeals to Community and Partnerships*, Oxford: Clarendon Press.

Crawford, A. (2008) 'Plural policing', in T. Newburn and P. Neyroud (eds) *Dictionary of Policing*, Cullompton: Willan.

Crawford, A. (2014) 'Police, policing and the future of the policing family', in J.M. Brown (ed) *The Future of Policing*, Abingdon: Routledge.

Crawford, A. and Lister, S. (2004) *The extended policing family: Visible patrols in residential areas*, Joseph Rowntree Foundation.

Crawford, A., Lister, S., Blackburn, S. and Burnett, J. (2005) *Plural Policing: The Mixed Economy of Visible Patrols in England and Wales*, Bristol: Policy Press.

Critchley, T.A. (1978) *A History of Police in England and Wales 900–1966*, London: Constable.

Curtis, T. and James, R. (2013) *Intensive Engagement: Smart Policing* [online] Available at: http://www.slideshare.net/curtistim/intensive-engagement-smart-policing-northampton-crimeprevention-summit-19-9-13 (Accessed 14 July 2016.)

Dalgleish, D. and Myhill, A. (2004) *Reassuring the Public: A Review of International Policing Interventions*, London: Home Office.

Dodd, T., Nicholas, S., Povey, D. and Walker, A. (2004) *Crime in England and Wales 2003/04. Home Office Statistical Bulletin 10/04.* ,ondon: Home Office.

Dunleavy, P. and O'Leary, B. (1987) *Theories of the State: The Politics of Liberal Democracy*, London: Macmillan.

Eaton, G. (2010) *The 'Big Society': New Doubts Emerge*, London: New Statesman.

Elliot, R. and Nicholls J. (1996) *It's Good to Talk: Lessons in Public Consultation and Feedback*, Police Research Group Paper 22, London: Home Office.

Emsley, C. (2014) 'Peel's principles, police principles', in J. Brown (ed) *The Future of Policing*, London: Routledge.

Fielding, N. (2009) *Getting the best out of community policing*, Police Foundation.

FitzGerald, M., Hough, M., Joseph, I. and Qureshi, T. (2002) *Policing for London*, Cullompton: Willan.

Flanagan, R. (2008a) *Her Majesty's Inspectorate of Constabulary: Serving Communities and Individuals*, London: Central Office of Information.

Flanagan, R. (2008b) *Lancashire Constabulary: Neighbourhood Policing Developing Citizen Focused Policing*, London: Central Office of Information.

Forrester, K., Chatterton, M. and Pease, K. (1988) *The Kirkholt Burglary Prevention Project, Rochdale*, Home Office Crime Prevention Unit Paper 23, London: Home Office.

Forrester, K., Frenz, S., O'Connell, M. and Pease, K. (1990) *The Kirkholt Burglary Project, Phase Two*, Home Office Crime Prevention Unit Paper 23, London: Home Office.

Foster, J. and Jones, C. (2010). ' "Nice to do" and Essential: Improving Neighbourhood Policing in an English Police Force.' *Policing: A journal of Policy and Practice* 4(4): 395–402

Fraser, C., Hagelund, C., Sawyer, K. and Stacey, M. (2014) 'The expert citizen, reform ideas', available at www.reform.uk/publication/the-expert-citizen (accessed 17 March 2016).

Frevel, B. (2015) 'Pluralisation of local policing in Germany: security between the state's monopoly of force and the market', *European Journal of Policing Studies*, vol 2, no 3, pp 267-84.

Friedman, R. (1992) *Community Policing: Comparative Perspectives and Prospects*, New York, NY: Prentice Hall.

Frinton (2015), available at www.telegraph.co.uk/news/uknews/law-and-order/11971625/Residents-of-seaside-town-pay-private-security-firm-100-a-week-to-police-streets.html

Fukuyama, F. (1999) *The Great Disruption: Human Nature and the Reconstitution of Social Order*, New York, NY: The Free Press.

Fukuyama, F. (2005), *State Building: Governance and World Order in the Twenty-First Century*, London, : Profile Books Ltd.

Garland, D. (1996) 'The limits of the sovereign state', *British Journal of Criminology*, vol 36, no 2, pp 445-471.

Garland, D. (2001) *The Culture of Control*, Oxford, Oxford University Press.

Gibbs, B. and Greenhalgh, B. (2014) 'The Police Mission in the twenty first century: rebalancing the role of the first public service', Reform Publication available at http://www.no-offence.org/pdfs/69.pdfhttp://www.no-offence.org/pdfs/69.pdf (accessed 22 November 2015).

Gill, M.L. and Mawby, R.I. (1990) *A Special Constable: A Study of the Police Reserve*, Aldershot: Averbury.

Goffman, E. (1990) *The Presentation of Self in Everyday Life*, London: Penguin.

Goldsmith, A. (2001) 'Pursuit of police integrity: leadership and governance dimensions', *Current Issues in Criminal Justice*, vol 13, p 185.

Goldstein, H. (1990) *Problem-Oriented Policing*, New York, NY: McGraw-Hill.

Gravelle, J. and Rogers, C. (2009a) 'The economy of policing: the impact of the volunteer', *Policing: A Journal of Policy and Practice,* vol 82, pp 10-13.

Gravelle, J. and Rogers, C. (2009b) 'Your country needs you: the economic viability of volunteers in the police', *Safer Communities: A Journal of Practice, Opinion, Policy and Research*, vol 8, no 3, pp 4-8

Greig-Midlane, J. (2014) *Changing the beat? The impact of austerity on the neighbourhood policing workforce,* Cardiff: Cardiff University Press.

Halpern, D. (2007) *Social Capital*, Cambridge: Polity Press.

Halpern, D. (2010) *The Hidden Wealth of Nations*, Cambridge: Polity Press.

Hartshill, H. (2015) 'Former Staffordshire Police officers offer families private police officers - for £1 a week', available at http://www.stokesentinel.co.uk/staffordshire-police-officers-offer-families/story-25854938-detail/story.html#ixzz4Cml7BSSk (accessed 25 November 2016)

Hauber, A., Hofstra, B., Toornvliet, L. and Zandbergen, A. (1996) 'Some new forms of functional social control in the Netherlands and their effects', *British Journal of Criminology*, vol 36, no 2, pp 199-219.

Hebson, G., Grimshaw, D. and Marchington, M.P. (2003) 'PPPs and the changing public sector ethos: case-study evidence from the health and local authority sectors', *Work, Employment and Society*, vol 17, no 3, pp 481-501.

Herbert, N. (2011) Speech to the National Community Safety Network Conference, available at www.bbc.co.uk/news/uk-34864781 (accessed 26 November 2015).

HMIC (Her Majesty's Inspectorate of Constabulary) (2001) *Open All Hours: A Thematic Inspection Report on the Role of Police Visibility and Accessibility in Public Reassurance*, London: HMIC.

HMIC (2008) *Serving Neighbourhoods and Individuals: A Thematic Report on Neighbourhood Policing and Developing Citizen Focus Policing*, London: HMIC.

HMIC (2012a) *Demanding Times*, London: HMIC.

HMIC (2012b) *Policing in austerity: One year on*, London: HMIC.

HMIC (2013) *Policing in Austerity: Rising to the Challenge*, London: HMIC.

HMIC (2014a) 'State of policing: the annual assessment of policing in England and Wales 2013/2014', available at www.justiceinspectorates. gov.uk/hmic (accessed 21 July 2015).

HMIC (2014b) *Policing in austerity: Meeting the challenge*, available at https://www.justiceinspectorates.gov.uk/hmic/wp-content/uploads/policing-in-austerity-meeting-the-challenge.pdf

HMIC (2015) 'PEEL: police efficiency 2015', available at www. justiceinspectorates.gov.uk/hmic/wp-content/uploads/peel-police-efficiency-2015.pdf (accessed 9 November 2015).

HM Treasury (2007) *Meeting the aspirations of the British people: 2007 Pre-Budget Report and Comprehensive Spending Review*, London: Stationery Office.

Hodge, G.A. and Greve, C. (2009) 'PPPs: the passage of time permits a sober reflection', *Economic Affairs*, March, pp 33-9.

Home Office (1984) *Crime Prevention Circular 8/1984*, London: HMSO.

Home Office (1989) *Tackling Crime*, London, HMSO.

Home Office (1990) *Circular 44/90, Crime Prevention: The Success of the Partnership Approach*, London: HMSO.

Home Office (1991) *Safer Communities: The Local Delivery of Crime Prevention through the Partnership Approach* (the Morgan report), London: HMSO.

Home Office (1994) *Partners Against Crime*, London: HMSO.

Home Office (1997) *Getting to Grips with Crime: A New Framework for Local Action. Examples of Local Authority Partnerships Activity*, London: HMSO.

Home Office (2001) *Policing a New Century: A Blueprint for Reform*, London, Home Office.

Home Office (2005a) *National Policing Plan 2005–2008*, London: The Stationery Office.

Home Office (2005b) *Building Communities, Beating Crime: A Better Police Service for the 21st Century*, London: The Stationery Office

Home Office (2006a) *From Policing the Local Beat to Disrupting Global Crime Networks: Reforming the Structure of Policing in the 21st Century*, London: The Stationery Office.

Home Office (2006b) *Citizen Focus: Good Practice Guide*. London: Home Office.

Home Office (2006c) *Crime and Cohesive Communities: Research, Development and Statistics – Communities Group*, London: Home Office, available at: http://rds.homeoffice.gov.uk/rds/pdfs06/rdsolr1906.pdf (accessed 23 September 2010).

Home Office (2008) *From the Neighbourhood to the National: Policing our Communities Together*, Cm 7448, London: The Stationery Office.

Home Office (2010a) *Policing in the 21st Century: Reconnecting the Police and the People*, London: The Stationery Office.

Home Office (2010b) *Policing: Police and Crime Commissioners*, London: The Stationery Office.

Home Office (2012) *Consultation on a Future Regulatory Regime for the Private Security Industry*, London: Home Office.

Home Office (2015a) 'Police workforce numbers, 31st March 2015', available at www.gov.uk/government/statistics/police-workforce-england-and-wales-31-march-2015-data-tables

Home Office (2015b) 'Reforming the powers of police staff and volunteers', available at www.gov.uk/government/uploads/system/uploads/attachment_data/file/459450/150909_Consultation_Document_on_Powers_of_Police_Staff_and_Volunteers__FINAL_.pdf (accessed 17 November 2015).

Hough, M., Jackson, J., Bradford, B., Myhill, A. and Quinton, P. (2010) 'Procedural justice, trust and institutional legitimacy', *Oxford Journal of Policing*, vol 4, no 3, pp 23–34

Hughes, G. (1996) 'Strategies of crime prevention and community safety in contemporary Britain', *Studies on Crime and Crime Prevention* 5, pp 221-44.

Hughes, G. (1998) *Understanding Crime Prevention*, Buckingham: Open University Press.

Hughes, G. (2007) *The Politics of Crime and Community*, Basingstoke: Palgrave Macmillan.

IFS (Institute for Fiscal Studies) (2015) 'The IFS green budget', available at www.ifs.org.uk/events/1110

Independent Police Commission (2013) *Policing for a Better Britain: Report of the Independent Police Commission*. London: Independent Police Commission.

Innes, M. (2003) *Understanding Social Control*, Maidenhead, Oxford University Press.

Innes, M. (2004) 'Signal crimes and signal disorders: notes on deviance as communication action', *British Journal of Sociology*, vol 55, no 3, pp 335-55.

Innes, M. (2007) 'The reassurance function', *Policing*, vol 1, no 2, pp 132-41.

Innes, M. (2014) *Signal Crimes. Social Reactions to Crime, Disorder and Control*, Oxford: Oxford University Press.

ITN (2010) 'What is the "Big Society" initiative?', available at http://itn.co.uk/59eb147bcb73391305d1226c9945aa69.html (accessed 26 August 2010).

IVR (Institute for Volunteering Research) (2003) 'Volunteer investment and value audit', available at www.ivr.org.uk/NR/rdonlyres/C07E99EC-3818-4618-A0DB-914ACAD28B65/0/viva2003.pdf (accessed 24 December 2008).

Jansson, K. (2006) *Black and minority ethnic groups' experiences and perceptions of crime: findings from the 2004/05 British Crime Survey*, London: Home Office Research Development and Statistics Directorate.

John, T. and Maguire, M. (2004) *The National Intelligence Model: Key Lessons from Early Research*, London: Home Office.

Johnston, L. (1992) *The Rebirth of Private Policing*, London: Routledge.

Johnston, L. (2005) 'From 'community' to 'neighbourhood' policing: Police Community Support Officers and the 'police extended family' in London', *Journal of Community and Applied Psychology*, 15(3) 241–54.

Johnston, L. and Shearing C. (2003) *The Governance of Security: Explorations in Policing and Justice*, London: Routledge.

Jones, T. (2008) 'The accountability of policing', in T. Newburn (ed) *The Handbook of Policing*, Cullompton: Willan.

Jones, T. and Newburn, T. (2002a) *Private Security and Private Policing*, Oxford: Oxford University Press.

Jones, T. and Newburn, T. (2002b) 'The transformation of policing', *British Journal of Criminology*, vol 42, no 1, pp 128-46.

Jones, T. and Newburn, T. (2006) *Plural Policing: A Comparative Perspective*, Abingdon: Routledge.

Jones, T. and Van Sluis, A. (2009) 'National standards, local delivery: police reform in England and Wales', *The Contested Police*, German Policy Studies, vol 5, no 2.

Kingston (2015), available at www.surreycomet.co.uk/ news/13875727._I_don_t_think_it_s_right___The_future_of_ Kingston_without_PCSOs

Klockars, C. (1985) *Idea of Police*, Beverly Hills, CA: Sage Publications.

Kretzmann, J.P. and McKnight, J.L. (1993) *Building Communities from the Inside Out: A Path toward Finding and Mobilizing a Community's Assets*, Evanston, IL: Institute for Policy Research.

Lee, W.L.M. (1901) *A History of Police in England*, Methuen: London.

Lentz, S.A. and Chaire R.H. (2007) 'The invention of Peel's principles: a study of policing text book history', *Journal of Criminal Justice*, vol 35, no 1, pp 69-79.

Lister, S. and Jones, T. (2015) 'Plural policing and the challenge of democratic accountability', in S. Lister and M. Rowe (eds) *Accountability of Policing*, Abingdon: Routledge.

Lloyd, K. and Foster, J. (2009) *Citizen Focus and Community Engagement: A Review of the Literature*, London: The Police Foundation.

Loader, I. (2000) 'Plural policing and democratic governance', *Social and Legal Studies*, vol 9, no 3, pp 323-45.

Local Government Association (2012) *Police and Crime Commissioners: A guide for councils*, available at http://www.local.gov.uk/c/ document_library/get_file?uuid=7aae958c-9da7-44ee-8ebc-9fe2d772fc0c&groupId=10180

Lowenthal, D. (2011) *The Past is a Foreign Country*, Cambridge: Cambridge University Press.

Manning, P.K. (1010) *Democratic Policing in a Changing World*, Boulder, CO: Paradigm.

Mastrofski, S. (1999) *Policing For People: Ideas in American Policing*, Washington, DC: Police Foundation.

May, T. (2010) 'Fight crime', available at www.gov.uk/government/ speeches/police-reform-theresa-mays-speech-to-the-police-federation (accessed 25 November 2015).

May, T. (2014) 'Police Federation crying wolf over cuts, says Theresa May', www.bbc.co.uk/news/uk-32806520 (accessed 22 May 2015).

McLaughlin, E. (2007) *The New Policing*, London: Sage Publications.

McLaughlin, E. and Muncie, J. (2006) *The Sage Dictionary of Criminology*, London: Sage Publications.

Millie, A. (2012) 'The policing task and the expansion (and contraction) of British policing', *British Journal of Criminology*, vol 52, no 6, pp 1092-112.

Morash, M. and Ford, J.K. (eds) (2002) *The move to community policing: Making change happen,* Sage Publications.

Morris, S. (1996) *Policing Problem Housing Estates*, Police Research Group Crime Detection and Prevention Paper 74, London: Home Office.

Morse, A. (2015) *Financial sustainability of police forces in England and Wales*, London: Home Office.

Myhill, A. (2006) *Community Engagement in Policing: Lessons from the Literature*, London: Home Office

National Debate Advisory Group (2015) 'Reshaping policing for the public', available at www.npcc.police.uk/documents/reports/Reshaping%20policing%20for%20the%20public.pdf (accessed 9 November 2015).

NCIS (National Criminal Intelligence Service) (2000) 'The National Intelligence Model', available at www.intelligenceanalysis.net/National%20Intelligence%20Model.pdf (accessed on 26 November 2015).

Neyroud, P. (2010) *Review of Police Leadership and Training*. Available at: https://www.gov.uk/government/uploads/system/uploads/attachment_data/file/118222/report.pdf. (Accessed 14 July 2016)

O'Brien, ? (2011) *Citizen Power in Peterborough: one year on*. Available at: https://www.thersa.org/discover/publications-and-articles/reports/interim-report---citizen-power-peterborough-one-year-on/ (accessed 14 July 2016).

OCSE (Organisation for Security and Cooperation Europe) (2008) *Guidebook on Democratic Policing*, Vienna: OCSE.

Office of the Police and Crime Commissioner Gloucestershire (2013) 'Police and crime plan 2013-2017', available at www.gloucestershire-pcc.gov.uk/wp.../PCP-Revision-201415-v1.doc (accessed 22 September 2014).

O'Neill, M. (2014a) 'Ripe for the chop or the public face of policing? PCSOs and neighbourhood policing in austerity', *Policing*, vol 8, no 3, pp 265-73.

O'Neill, M. (2014b) 'Playing nicely with others', in J.M. Brown (ed) *The Future of Policing*, Abingdon: Routledge.

O'Neill, M. (2015) 'Police community support officers in England: a dramaturgical analysis', *Policing and Society: An International Journal of Research and Policy*, available at www.tandfonline.com/doi/pdf/10.1080/10439463.2015.1020805

Ostrom, E., Parks, R.B., Whitaker, G.P. and Percy, S.L. (1978) 'The public service production process: a framework for analysing police services', *Police Studies Journal*, vol7, pp 381-9.

PA Consulting (2001) *Diary of a Police Officer*, Home Office Research Report 149, London: Home Office.

Palmer, S.H. (1990) *Police and Protest in England and Ireland, 1780-1850*, Cambridge: Cambridge University Press.

Palmiotto, M.J. (2013) *Community Policing: A Police Citizen Partnership*, Abingdon: Routledge.

Pearce, S. (2015) 'Degrees of training', *Police Professional*, no 477, October, pp 14-17.

Peak, K.J. and Glensor, R.W. (1996) *Community Policing and Problem Solving: Strategies and Practices*, Upper Saddle River, NJ: Prentice Hall.

Pearson, G., Blagg, H., Smith, D., Sampson, A. and Stubbs, P. (1992) 'Crime, community and conflict: the multi-agency approach', in D. Downes (ed) *Unravelling criminal justice*, Palgrave Macmillan, pp 46-72.

Pirie, M. (1998) 'The millennium generation', available at www.adamsmith.org/sites/default/files/images/uploads/publications/millennial-generation.pdf (accessed 26 November 2015).

Police Federation (2014) 'Beat Bobbies an endangered species, says Police Federation', available at www.bbc.co.uk/news/uk-32807479 (accessed 22 May 2015).

Police Foundation. (2014) *Does neighbourhood policing have a future?*. Oxford Policing Policy Forum, 16.

Prenzler, T. (2013) *Outsourcing of Policing Tasks: Scope and Prospects*, Sydney: Australian Security Industry.

Prenzler, T. and Wakefield, A. (2009) 'Privatization', in A. Wakefield and J. Fleming (eds) *The Sage Dictionary of Policing*, London: Sage Publications, pp 244-6.

Punch, M. (2011) *Shoot to Kill: Police, Firearms and Fatal Force*, Bristol: Policy Press.

Putnam, R.D. (2000) *Bowling Alone*, London: Simon & Schuster.

Radzinowicz, L. (1956) *A History of English Civil Law and its Administration from 1750*, London: Stevens and Sons.

Reiner, R. (2007) *Law and Order: An Honest Citizen's Guide to Crime and Control*, Cambridge: Polity Press.

Reiner, R. (2010) *The Politics of the Police* (4th edn), Oxford: Oxford University Press.

Reiner, R. (2013) 'Who governs? Democracy, plutocracy, science and prophecy in policing', *Criminology and criminal justice*, vol 13, no 2, pp 161-180.

Reith, C. (1956) *A New Study of Police History*, London: Oliver and Boyd.

Rogers, C. (2004) 'From Dixon to Z Cars: the introduction of unit beat Policing in England and Wales', *Police History Journal*, no 19, pp 10-14.

Rogers, C. (2012) *Crime Reduction Partnerships*, Oxford: Oxford University Press.

Rogers, C. and Gravelle, J. (2012) 'UK policing and change: reflections for policing worldwide', *Review of European Studies*, vol 4, no 1, pp 42-51.

Rogers, C. and Milliner, A. (2010) 'The Big Society: ladders of engagement', *Police Professional*, no 228, 28 October.

Rowland, R. and Coupe, T. (2013) 'Patrol officers and public reassurance: a comparative evaluation of police officers, PCSOs, ACSOs and private security guards', *Policing and Society: An International Journal of Research and Policy*, available at www.tandfonline.com/doi/pdf/10.1080/10439463.2013.784300

Roycroft, M. (2014) 'A blended model for the public-private provision of policing for England and Wales' in The Future of Policing. [Coventry University ebrary] ed. by Brown, J. Oxon: Routledge. Available at: http://site.ebrary.com/lib/coventry/reader.action?docID=10779072(Accessed 14 July 2016)

Savage, S. (2007) *Police reform: Forces for change*, Oxford: Oxford University Press.

Scarman, Lord (1981) *The Brixton Disorders*, London: HMSO.

Security Industry Authority (2016) Review document, available at www.gov.uk/government/consultations/review-of-the-security-industry-authority-sia (accessed 17 March 2016).

Shearing, C.D. and Stenning, P.C. (1981) 'Modern private security: its growth and implications', in M. Tonry and N. Morris (eds) *Crime and Justice: An Annual Review of Research, Vol 3*, Chicago, IL: University of Chicago Press.

Shearing, C.D. and Stenning, P.C. (1983) 'Private security: implications for social control', *Social Problems*, vol 30, no 5, pp 498-505.

Sinclair, M. and Taylor, C. (2008) *The Cost of Crime*, London: TaxPayers' Alliance.

Skinns, L. (2008) 'A prominent participant? The role of the state in police partnerships: review essay) *Policing & Society*, vol 18, no 3, pp 311-321.

Sklansky, D.A. (2008) *Democracy and the Police*, Stanford, CA: Stanford University Press.

Skogan, W. (1990) *Disorder and Decline: Crime and the Spiral of Decay in American Neighbourhoods*, New York, NY: Free Press.

Skogan, W. (1992) *Impact of Policing on Social Disorder: Summary of Findings*, Washington, DC: US Department of Justice, Office of Justice Programs.

Skogan, W. (1998) 'The police and the public', in H. Schwind, E. Kube and H. Kuhune (eds) *Festschrift für Hans Joachim Schneider*, Berlin and New York: Walter de Gruyter.

Skogan, W. (2006a) 'Asymmetry in the impact of encounters with police', *Policing and Society*, vol 16, no 2, pp 99-126.

Skogan, W.G. (2006b) 'The promise of community policing', in D. Weisburd and A. Braga (eds) *Police Innovation: Contrasting Perspectives*, New York, NY: Cambridge University Press

Stoker, G. (2006) *Why Politics Matters: Making Democracy Work*, Basingstoke: Palgrave Macmillan.

Stead, P.J. (1985) *The Police of Britain*, London: Macmillan.

Stenning, P.C. and Shearing, C.D. (1981) 'Modern private security: its growth and implications', in M. Tonry and N. Morris (eds) *Crime and Justice: An Annual Review of research, Vol 3*, Chicago, IL: University of Chicago Press.

Stenning, P.C. and Shearing, C.D. (1983) 'Private security: implications for social control', *Social Problems*, vol 30, no 5, pp 498-505.

Stenning, P. and Shearing, C. (2015) 'Privatisation, Pluralisation and the Globalisation of Policing', *Research Focus*, vol 3, pp 1-8.

Storch, R. (1975) 'The plague of the blue locusts: police reform and popular resistance in Northern England, 1840–57, *International Revue of Social History*, Vol 20.

Sunshine, J. and Tyler, T.R. (2003) 'The role of procedural justice and legitimacy in shaping public support for policing', *Law and Society Review*, vol 37, no 93, pp 555-89.

Taylor, M. and Travis, A. (2012) 'G4S chief predicts mass police privatisation', www.theguardian.com/uk/2012/jun/20/g4s-chief-mass-police-privatisation (accessed 16 November 2015).

Terpstra, J. and Van Stokkom, B. (2015) 'Plural policing in comparative perspective: four models of regulation', *European Journal of Policing Studies*, vol 2, no 3, pp 325-43.

Terpstra, J., Van Stokkom, B. and Spreeuwers, R. (2013) *Who Patrols the Streets?*, The Hague: Eleven International Publishing.

Tilley, N. (1993) *The Prevention of Crime against Small Businesses: The Safer Cities Experience*, Police Research Group Crime Detection and Prevention Paper 45, London: Home Office.

Tiptree (2015) available at www.dailymail.co.uk/news/article-3294436/The-Essex-village-hiring-security-squad-Residents-Tiptree-force-act-police-force-says-getting-rid-beat-officers.html

Tobias, J.J. (1979) *Crime and Police in England, 1700–1900*, Dublin: Gill and Macmillan.

Trojanowicz, R.C. (1983) *An Evaluation of the Neighbourhood Foot Patrol Program in Flint, Michigan*, Flint, MI: Michigan State University Press.

Trojanowicz, R.C. and Bucqueroux, B. (1990) *Community Policing and How to Get Started*, Abingdon: Routledge.

Tyler, T.R. (2003) 'Procedural justice, legitimacy and the effective rule of law', in M. Tonry (ed) *Crime and Justice: A Review of Research, 30*, Chicago, IL: University of Chicago Press.

Tyler, T.R. and Huo, Y.J. (2002) *Trust in the Law: Encouraging Public Cooperation with the Police and Courts*, New York, NY: Russell Sage Foundation.

UNODC (United Nations Office on Drugs and Crime) (2011) 'Civilian private security services: their role, oversight and contribution to crime prevention and community safety', available at www.unodc.org/documents/justice-and-prison-reform/Expert-group-meeting-Bangkok/IEGMCivilianPrivateSecurity/UNODC_CCPCJ_EG.5_2011_1_English.pdf (accessed 26 November 2015).

Van Dijk, A., Huogewoning, F. and Punch, M. (2015) *What Matters in Policing: Change, Values and Leadership in Turbulent Times,* Bristol: Policy Press.

Van Steden, R. (2007) *Privatising Policing: Describing and Explaining the Growth of Private Security*, The Hague: Boom Juridische Uitgevers.

Van Steden, R. and Sarre, R. (2007) 'The Growth of Privatized Policing: Some Cross-national Data and Comparisons', *International Journal of Comparative and Applied Criminal Justice*, vol 31, no 1, pp51-71.

Waddington P.A.J. (1999) *Policing Citizens*, London: UCL Press.

Wakefield, A. (2009) 'Pluralisation', in A. Wakefield and J. Fleming (eds) *The Sage Dictionary of Policing*, London: Sage Publications, pp 227-9.

White, A. (2015) 'The politics of police privatisation: a multiple streams approach', *Criminology and Criminal Justice*, vol 15, no 3, pp 283-99.

Zedner, L. (2006) 'Policing before and after the police: the historical antecedents of contemporary crime control', *British Journal of Criminology*, vol 46, no 1, pp 78-96.

Index

Reference to figures and tables are shown in *italics*